The Mo

Deer Hunting Yarns of New Zealand

By Clive Sutton
Compiled and edited by
Albert David Sutton

First edition 2012

Cover design by A. D. Sutton

ISBN 978-1480025332

Contents

Foreword
By Albert David Sutton

As a boy, growing up with a father who was the consummate hunter, I was left with the enduring memory of a man who would have the lounge, garage or car packed with rifles, tents, sleeping bags and packs ready for yet another hunting trip. I would awake in the morning to find him gone, sometimes for a few days and sometimes for more than a week. He would return dirty, smelly and unshaven with a big smile, especially if he had shot a deer or a trophy head.

There would be plastic bags of blood red meat for the freezer along with heads and pelts, which he would boil, tan and preserve to mount along our fence or over the garage. On weekends and holidays when he wasn't hunting we would be packed into the car and driven to any of the rifle ranges around Auckland to spend the day shooting targets and socialising with the large group of hunters and shooters who were the NZDA (New Zealand Deerstalkers Association).

Albert Clive Sutton, known as Clive, was made a life member of the South Auckland branch of the NZDA on 15 February 1995. Before that time he spent many years working as Secretary and Editor of the Association's monthly publication The Bush Telegraph for which he would also contribute articles on his knowledge of hunting, shooting and rifle safety and short stories of his expeditions. It is the latter of these that I have collected here.

Clive was what we would term 'a real kiwi bloke' whose interests were in hunting, fishing, rugby, cars and beer. He refereed rugby games and began to climb the refereeing ladder for the Auckland Rugby Union until illness and a heart bypass forced him to give it up. Hunting, though, was not something he would relinquish, because the New Zealand bush was his mistress, and in later years he and his mates took to using 4 x 4 Quad Bikes to get around on. I think, in those last years, it became less about stalking deer and more about being in the bush, for which he built his own hut (see 'Car Case Creek') for himself and his hunting buddies.

In memory of Albert Clive Sutton (two minutes to midnight 31 December 1934–2002).

The Motu Mob

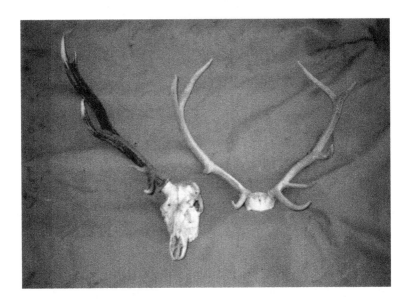

It had been a little over 6 hours since this party of five Auckland hunters had turned their backs on 'Festus' the Land Rover and now, in drizzling rain, stood looking down into the part of the Motu River that was to be their range for the next eight days. As usual the last 200 metres of the journey proved to be the most difficult. Interlaced tangles of supple jack took on the characteristics of a loosely wound ball of string, through which you had to force yourself and your pack, which by this stage threatened to wrench your shoulders apart at the point where your neck was attached to them.

Thankfully the camp site was reached and the packs were lowered to the ground with audible sighs of relief. Five months of planning and dreaming had preceded this trip, and here we were at last, pitching our camp with nightfall approaching and a week of good hunting ahead.

Intentionally the only meat on the trip's grocery list was two pounds of bangers for the first night's meal. All further slabs of protein were hoped to be gained from the surrounding bush. Dennis produced a fishing line from his pack along with a few rashers of bacon which had been rescued from that morning's brekky. We were rewarded only minutes later with one extremely large eel that could solve our meat problems for days ahead if required.

After gorging ourselves on the snarlers, five very weary hunters disappeared into their sleeping bags, and in no time were fast asleep. Being winter, when the nights are longer than the days, all hands were on deck at first light and, after a feed of eel, began to prepare for that long awaited appointment with Mr Red Deer. Even though this trip had been organised to coincide with the rut, our first concern for the day was to provide meat for the camp.

Myself and Chris, who was Noj's first son aged 13 years, made an assault on the ridge behind camp with Les (Noddy) and his 7mm forming a rear guard. Noj and Dennis elected to go back across the river and test their skills on that side of the valley.

We had hardly settled into stalking mode when a large hind wandered into view, apparently responding to my inviting imitation of a stag's roar. My little .308 did its job well and young Chris had seen his first wild deer after only 10 minutes of hunting. He then eagerly helped with the dressing out and transportation of the carcass back to camp.

Noddy arrived on the scene during this exercise, and as we stood talking over the event, a shot boomed out from across the river.

We found out later that Noj had given a pig a frontal

lobotomy with his 30.06 and this was photographed by a jubilant Chris, the pig astride his father's shoulders as he waded the river back to camp, an hour or so later. Dennis continued on his own and was not sighted again until well after dark had fallen. He had covered a huge slice of real estate during the day and had been rewarded with a very impressive 10 pointer.

After climbing high up on a ridge he said he had heard two stags arguing some way off and decided he would check out the fellow with the most authoritative voice. After hours of exhausting work, in this most difficult of country, he got a look at the cause of all the commotion only to be bitterly disappointed in what he saw. Leaving that one to live another day he turned his attention to the weaker sounding one.

This fellow proved to be a very different and impressive beast and he downed it with one shot from his .270. The trip back became quite perilous when darkness fell. In desperation he took to the river, complete with rifle, pack, antlers and cape, and proceeded to stumble, float and swim back downstream to camp. But it must have been worth the effort as four green eyed hunters pawed over his trophy. While Dennis put on some dry clothes and tucked into a large helping of venison stew the rest of us filled him in on our own day of hunting.

It seemed like a dream. After only one day we had scored a hind, one porker and a 10 point stag. We all wondered if it was too good to be true. The next day found the party scattered to all points of the compass. Plenty of pigs were seen. In fact the area seemed to be infested with them, but we left them alone.

Day three and Noj decided he and Chris would put in a big hike to try and bag a trophy. After a rather strenuous sidling of the river's faces he decided to cross over and seek greener pastures. Leaving Chris at the river's edge he made a sortie up a distinct ridge which was later to become known as 'The

Staircase'. On his way up he was shaken into action by a hind that raced across his path affording him only one quick shot, that served only to hasten the animal's flight.

Reprimanding himself for stirring up the wildlife over such a slim target he wondered whether it was worth continuing on up the ridge. He felt his chances had now dropped considerably after all that racket. But, finally, deciding he had nothing to lose, he carried on. Imagine his surprise then when after only a few moments a stag roared from not too far ahead.

He paused to calm his jangling nerves and, of all things, change the type of ammo in his magazine. Cautiously he eased himself over towards where Mr Red should be when suddenly, unbelievably, there he was. A stag of huge dimensions slightly to the left of the trail and lying down facing away from him.

Silently Noj brought his 30.06 to his shoulder and put the crosshairs to the animal's chest. As if by instinct the animal lunged to its feet and turned, looking directly at him, forcing Noj to breathlessly readjust his aim and touch off the shot. The Stag lurched for a few metres and then crashed to the forest floor after taking another round in the shoulder.

Hastening over he counted 11 points on a magnificently shaped set of antlers.

By now the daylight hours were diminishing and he hastened back down the ridge under the weight of his large prize to rejoin Chris, splashing across the river to the boy who waited patiently for his return. But it seemed that Chris had his own wild tale to tell when he finally reached his side.

He said that some time after his father had left him he had heard a movement in the bush at his back, so he lay low on the river bank. From his vantage point he saw a large brown shape move through the dense cover toward him and his first thoughts were to reach for his little instamatic camera. Sliding it from his day pack the unsuspecting stag made its way to the water's edge only metres from where the excited youngster lay.

He took his picture in quick time, afraid the monster might suddenly disappear, when of all things, it turned its head to look the photographer clean in the eye before continuing on with its refreshment. The animal seemed in no real hurry and Chris had ample time to count the 12 even points and even take a second and third photograph before the big fellow turned, and at an even leisurely pace, departed. All these events were then related to three wide eyed mates back at camp.

Now at this time of year one would expect it to be cold and yet this was far from the case and the quantity of blowflies bore testament to the mild conditions. They could be relied upon to deposit large clumps of eggs upon anything remotely woollen. Swannis, sox, singlets, balaclavas, everything came in for their attention and, worst of all, the meat was almost impossible to protect.

Noj, in fact, had one alarming incident while out hunting. He had a persistent itch in the region of his naval and diving his hand down inside his singlet retrieved one very healthy maggot. The eggs in his singlet were hatching and the procedure was repeated several times that day. He remarked that he was the only one in camp with sense enough to cart fresh meat around with him.

After witnessing all these fine trophies being brought back into camp I decided I would have to get my act together and made a resolution that the next day would be my turn. Soon after daybreak Noddy and I were to be found making progress upstream from camp. The cloud was hanging well down in the valley and the river's banks were very steep and rocky necessitating many crossings of its wide deep and, at times, swift waters.

After an hour, the last of our planned crossings lay before us, as did our destination. Picking our way across we found ourselves at the foot of The Staircase, up which we had been strongly advised to go for our day of hunting. Another 45 minutes and we had progressed to a point about 300 metres above the river when a lone roar was heard from directly across the stream and at a slightly higher elevation than ours. A minute or two later and the respondent answered my roar giving away his approximate location.

He was showing signs of continuing his bellowing for a while, and with visions of Chris's 12 pointer in mind, we retraced our steps, plunging back into that river with the greasy bottom and climbing up towards where we thought our target to be. Since descending from the opposite ridge we had not heard another sound from the stag, but this was to be expected, as the river's rumble would have drowned out any noise from him anyway.

But once away from the river, and at about 11am, we stepped into a small grassy clearing on a high saddle. Still we had yet to hear a sound so decided that this was a good place to take a break and took our time munching on some watercress sandwiches. Just as our thoughts had relaxed from the business of hunting the peace and quiet was shattered with the roar of a stag only metres away.

I glanced at Noddy knowing that what I saw on his face must reflect my own and almost before we could speak there came another roar. Not a full throttled bellowing roar but rather the sound of an animal letting his immediate neighbours know that he was around and in charge of this neck of the woods.

We now knew him to be on the other side of the saddle where the ridge took off at an acute angle toward a high peak towering above us from the north. Using only the front soles of our boots we made slow progress toward our target that now seemed to become more upset with each step we took. At last he could be pinpointed and was found to be in command of a small knoll up ahead.

After getting the okay from Noddy I took off on my own towards the stag who had not the slightest hint of our presence and was busy thrashing the undergrowth with his antlers while now maintaining an almost constant stream of groans and growls. Only metres separated us but still he remained concealed by the heavy undergrowth, except for the odd glimpse of an antler, which was useless as a target.

Then without warning he moved off to my right and for one awful moment it appeared that he may wander completely out of sight. Then it happened, he altered his course a little and swung towards me, still thrashing and growling. I knew I would have to get a shot at him soon because the distance between us was closing with every step he took and I feared the whole deal could turn into hand to hoof combat. I put my rifle to my shoulder and watched through the scope at the patch of vegetation where I anticipated he would appear.

Finally he burst into view mere metres away and was just a blur in the scope. His head was down near the ground swiping back and forwards as I placed the crosshairs between his shoulder blades and fired. The fleeting glimpse I got of the animal, as the recoil spoilt the picture, was of him lunging to his left off the side of the ridge.

Stoking a fresh round into the breach I leapt to the edge in time to see him sliding tail first down the incline to end up draped around a ponga. So true to form, my little Mod 600 Remington .308 hadn't let me down and only the one shot had been required to bag him.

With only one thought in mind I slid down to his side to take a look at his rack. He was the largest deer I had ever seen either in or out of captivity but he was also the biggest disappointment of my stalking life, as I now saw that this magnificent fellow, sported only one antler. But what an antler it was and, had it boasted a counterpart, would have compared most favourably with those back at camp.

Close inspection revealed that he had been without the missing antler for some considerable time. In fact the skull around the spot showed damage that would have taken at least a couple of years to heal and it looked almost deformed. I decided to claim the head regardless, at least as evidence of my tale.

The path back to camp was pathed with profanities as I cursed and cursed again my misfortune. We paused briefly to collect some watercress from a small stream and arrived back at The Motel for afternoon tea. The term 'motel' had replaced 'camp' some days earlier as each day saw another mod-con in the form of mushrooms from the vicinity collected and prepared in impeccable meals more akin to restaurant fodder.

Imagine for a moment a huge pot filled to the brim with a stew of export quality venison back steak, lightly browned, garnished and curried. A huge salad of fresh watercress, peas, beans and a liberal helping of potatoes mashed with butter. Afterwards this was followed by a large helping of creamed rice and raisins topped with apricots, and later still, a snack of prime venison liver sliced thinly, floured and fried in butter and eaten with the fingers for supreme appreciation.

This country we were in was so difficult to move around in that there was just no way meat could be taken home. There was already enough of a problem just getting yourself and the important gear out. That evening, after some discussion, we christened my lone antlered monster Cyclops.

The following day, with the weather still fine and warm, we

all departed The Motel shortly after daybreak. Dennis went off to look for Chris's 12 pointer while Noj and Chris decided to have another encounter with The Staircase. Noddy and I covered a fair amount of terra firma with only the one excursion towards a very vocal stag. But this had to be aborted due to the impossible nature of the terrain.

For Dennis however, things were going a little kinder and after pushing his way up a filthy razorback ridge he came to a small clearing on a saddle strewn with the remnants of skin and jaw bone he realised must have been from my kill the day before. With no set plan in mind he stood his ground for a good 20 minutes just admiring the view from this high perch.

A stag roared a little further up the ridge giving his hunting instincts a jab in the ribs and pulling him back from idle contemplation. Picking his way carefully upward, he passed, unknown to him, within a few metres of yesterday's carcass and continued climbing to take on this new challenger. Only 20 metres further up he got his first glimpse of a stag standing behind a tree with its rear flanks and a portion of its back showing.

He realised the animal could become aware of his presence at any moment and that only a stride or two would see the stag disappear out of sight, perhaps forever. He decided on a quick shot at the spine, which in his usual professional manner he hit, but the animal needed a second shot to finish it. This stag too proved to be of the same high standard as his earlier trophy, sporting 10 points and scoring over 250 on the Douglas scale. Dennis, being a man of deeds and few words had the story wrung out of him that night.

The following day an exercise was put into place whereby I might have been able to get a shot at a stag that was known to be on one particular ridge. Noj climbed up the nose to one side of the target stag while Dennis went up the ridge opposite. Between the two of them they started a roaring competition which it was hoped would get the fellow on my ridge started.

The whole deal became a waste of time however and the return down river became a carefree affair with Les capping off the adventure in fine form. He suddenly disappeared mid sentence high on a rocky outcrop as the shelf gave way beneath him and he descended in a flurry of arms and legs, complete with pack and rifle, into a deep pool in the river below. Noj and I were both roaring with laughter well before Les broke the surface.

Les reappeared in short time speaking a language that neither of us could understand as we waited for him to claw his way unassisted back up the rock face. The remainder of that journey was punctuated by peels of raucous laughter as the vision of Les's descent into the river kept returning. He stated later that he merely thought he had seen a deer swimming in the pool and had gone down to check.

Late that afternoon the weather, for the first time this trip, threatened to turn sour and we decided to move out the next day. Nightfall indeed brought the rain which gradually became heavier. Breakfast was eaten in the wet, under grey clouds that had settled on the valley as a fog. The journey back to civilisation was one of those unforgettable trips with the supplejack constantly entwining our packs and our trophy antlers. The rain soaked us to the skin before the top of the first big pull was even reached and the cold, which we had not felt all week, now permitted only the briefest of rest stops.

On the final downward leg of the journey the party was spread over a considerable distance as the weight in our packs took their toll. One by one, faces were to lighten up as they rounded the last bend to be greeted by the sight of Festus's steely tailgate waiting to welcome us back after its nine-day lone vigil. Our feet threatened to float us away now that the weight of our packs was removed and the gear was hastily stowed. Five very tired but very satisfied hunters cast their eyes homeward.

P.S. This event took place in 1973 and the four of us were to hunt that area every April for the next 5 years. Eventually the place, despite its remoteness, became too popular for our comfort and this particular trip remained as the most success-ful. It should be noted also that 6 kms on the map equaled 7 hours of weighty tramping and our little group would eventu-ally become known as "The Motu Mob."

Tania

For some time she had been making noises of how she would like to go on a hunting trip and, certainly, for quite a while her scores on the range had been on the improve. So much so that she had now attained the stage of winning the NZDA National Shoot for Women and for Juniors, as well as giving her father, who was one of the country's best shots, a big hurry up. So she seemed to think that it was time to test her skill on stalking a live target.

Her name was Tania and I decided to volunteer to escort her on her first ever hunting trip. The area I selected was my own pet spot and hence its location was a closely guarded secret. Lance and Carl, two of the younger club members, were also invited along to make up the party and Tania was given a fair amount of ribbing in the weeks leading up to the hunt of how she was going to have to gut out any kill. Not only that, the boys were also keen to show her how to strap up a stag, so she could carry it back to camp.

Easter weekend fell late in March and although it was a bit early for the roar, I had selected it for the hunt because it would not interfere with my own planned trip a couple of weeks later. Eastern Bay Trappers of Murupara were engaged to fly us in with their helicopter on a day when the weather was magnificent, giving Tania a superb view of the area we would be stalking.

Upon our arrival at the hut she was given the full tour of inspection, including the ensuite that was about 30 metres away and very smelly. The nearest running water was about 100 metres away down a slippery track on the other side of the hut.

A firewood working bee was held almost immediately and lengths of timber from a nearby wind-fallen tree were carted back to the hut to be chopped and stacked in the woodbox. There were three axes in action and Tania was given the job of picking up the split pieces and taking them into the hut. An inspection of the woodbox later revealed that she had buried the broom under a metre of firewood, so the hut did not get a sweep out until the final morning.

It soon became time for a hunt and Tania and I went for a stroll up the hut stream. After about half an hour we cut off up a spur to the ridge top and worked our way back towards camp. It was quite an easy stroll really though she seemed to think she had just scaled Mount Egmont. Now I have never been known to break any records going uphill, but with Tania in tow it was almost relaxing.

Downhill was the same, but in this direction she seemed to

prefer traversing the steeper spots on the seat of her pants while wearing a big grin. Crossing windfalls was also an education as it seems women have a secret gusset installed somewhere that allows them to scramble over fallen logs with a freedom that men do not possess.

In camp there was never any problem when it came to dish-washing time, but she seemed to insist that the blackened outside of all the pots and billies should be scrubbed clean. It took some time to convince her of the folly of that exercise, but she finally settled on accepting that deerstalkers do not like bright and shiny billies, on the outside anyway.

I was also treated to another first on this hunting trip. One night a floral arrangement of ragwort, thistle and crown fern appeared. It sprang from the centre of a used toilet roll and sat on the mantle piece. In the morning Easter Eggs were also found to be mysteriously deposited in our mugs.

On the final evening the three youngsters took to the rum, helping themselves until the bottle was dry, and in the end Lance fared the worst of their partying mood. He spent a very restless night and at one point I was awoken when he found a new and quicker way to descend to the floor from his top bunk.

Unfortunately the weekend came and went without sighting that live target we were after, though we were treated to the sound of one stag roaring steadily in the next watershed, all that final afternoon and again on the morning of our departure.

Perhaps the main difference between this trip and most others was the fact that moderate language was used the whole time and that a few extra paces had to be taken away from the hut when one went outside to strain the spuds.

Tania had occupied the front seat of the chopper on the way

in so I decided she could occupy 'Jim's Seat' in the back on the way out. As we neared the landing pad at Murupara I gave Derek a little nudge and wink, motioning to the occupants in the rear. He read my mind well enough because as he flew in over the pad he reared up and executed a very steep banked turn that had Tania staring down at the ground with only the door of the chopper separating her from a 100-metre free fall.

The look on her face as she sat surrounded by packs, billies and rifles was priceless, and was for me the highlight of the trip. It was too bad we couldn't bag a deer, but I promised her there would be a next time.

Percy

An old mate of mine, whom I had known since I was knee high to a grass hopper, and who chose to live hermit like out in the back blocks of the remote King Country, managed to secure himself a live suckling pig while he was out hunting. It was just the thing, he thought, to fatten up and butcher at a later date. However, the inevitable happened and by the time 'Percy', as he had become known, attained the desired size for carving, he was instead granted a reprieve because a certain affection had grown between the two. Now since this pig was to be spared the dinner plate my mate decided that he had to earn his keep, so he started riding him about the property like a horse.

There were, from time to time, some short bursts of bad temper from Percy but, on the whole, this activity proved acceptable. At some point my mate rode Percy, who was by now tipping 400lb, over to a neighbouring opossum trappers one afternoon for a chat. Four half gallon jars of home brew later it was time to get going but Percy was nowhere to be found.

Upon scouting the property my mate found the pig about 300 metres away rooting under a log, so he hopped onto his back and, reprimanding him strongly, turned him towards home by pulling on his ear.

Well the pig threw a fit and my mate had one hell of a job getting him going in the right direction. He finally succeeded and, after a rather contemptuous journey back, turned him into the gate of his home only to find to his amazement that the real Percy lay sprawled out on the verandah of his cabin.

A Nine Point Starter

The pile of gear that was still on the ground alongside the helicopter was beginning to look larger than the space left for me in the back of the D Model 500 beside, around and over where I was to sit. Four of us had made this trip, Gary, Brian, Jim and myself, and we were on our way from Murupara for five days of hunting in the Ureweras.

It was the first week of April and with half an ounce of luck the stags should be roaring. Amazingly the last morsel of gear was forced in and the door squeezed shut, sealing me into an immovable position which I was going to have to hold until our destination was reached. A minute or two later and we were airborne and it wasn't long before a slight twitch in my left leg threatened to turn into full blown cramp. My concern was, if that should happen, that I would end up booting Jim, who sat in front of me, out of the machine. But fortunately by twisting slightly to my right within the vice-like grip of all that gear I managed to get the thing to behave itself.

From a distance our first sight of the bivvy revealed what appeared to be towels pegged out on the clothesline, and although the door was closed, the place had an air about it that said it was occupied. We landed without anyone showing themselves and Jim quickly ducked under the rotors and skipped up to the hut to check it out, but all was okay and in no time at all the machine was unloaded and on its way once more.

There was a feeling of excitement as we made trip after trip from hut to helipad ferrying the gear inside. The hut book revealed that there had not been a hunter near the place for some months which was why the grass had grown so long around the doorway and beyond.

It had been an exhausting day up to this point, as we had all been awake since 4am, and after settling ourselves in we decided to take a nap to recuperate and then hit the trail for a hunt later in the afternoon. It must have been about 1pm, or thereabouts, when my slumber was disturbed by Garry saying, 'What's making that moaning noise?'

Now Garry could probably count all of his previous hunting trips on one hand, with this being his first ever foray into a Red Roar expedition. I lay there quietly listening for a couple of moments until a familiar roar wafted into the hut from a stag who was not too far away. With that, Brian came streaking (well almost, he still had his shirt on) up to the hut from the long drop to say there was a stag roaring up the creek by the dunny.

So hasty preparations were made to go and deal with this

fellow, but for one reason or another, we failed to surround him and he went silent. Brian decided to persist with stalking the beast while Garry and I wandered back to the hut clearing and just stood in the silence looking up into the bush that surrounded us.

To our surprise a stag roared upstream, this time on the far side, and then another answered from downstream, and not at all that far away either. I decided to join in and gave a couple of bars on my own roaring horn and got an immediate reply from the customer to our right. I motioned for Garry to follow me and we crossed the creek and proceeded to climb a nose, from where I had plucked a couple of porkers on a previous trip. About 30 metres up, the ridge benched off for a little way making for an excellent spot from which to look, listen and roar. One decent yodel from me received an immediate reply from within the basin alongside us. Then another came from the same direction but higher up, and lo and behold a third from across the stream behind us. Our eyes must had been wide as yet a fourth then roared from downstream of him.

After a minute or two of roaring abuse at one another it became clear that the joker low down in the basin was intent on keeping up the argument for a while yet so I sent Garry off in his direction to see if he could get a shot at him. The roaring was tit for tat as I continued arguing the point, with the other three stags chipping in now and again just to make the whole event a bit more exciting than it was. I was beginning to wonder where Garry had got to when I realised that the target animal was getting louder and closer.

I began making preparations, checking I was loaded and moving closer to the edge of the bench from where I could look down into the bush, and the direction I could expect him to approach from. Visibility was good and I could see all the way down the face, almost to the floor of the basin. I was still wondering just where Garry was when BOOM! The sound of a shot from his direction was followed by the sound of crashing scrub. It continued for a moment and then, silence. I waited for a minute or two and called out, 'Did you get him?'

'I think so,' was the reply.

'Did you hit him?'

'I think so?'

'Is there any blood?' I asked,baffled by his answers.

'I'm looking.'

There was silence for a while as he searched around. Then finally, 'Yep I've found some blood,' he called.

Right about now I was having some negative thoughts as Gary was hunting with a .250-300, which is not the sort of calibre I would immediately recommend to tackle a big Red Stag with.

Arriving on the scene I was shown a large patch of blood you could not hide with a 40 gallon drum, but oddly there were only a few odd drops leading away from the area for a pace or two, and then nothing. At my request Garry re-enacted the opera and we went over and over the ground looking for the bleeding stag until finally we spotted him. He had gone about another 10 paces and had jumped over a log, keeled over and then slid back down behind it, leaving only about 10 centimetres of one antler visible.

He turned out to be a 5 x 4 nine pointer and nothing that was going to break any records but he was one that will never be forgotten by Garry. The stag was big as far as bulk goes and it took a fair amount of puffing and grunting to extract him from behind the log. In time we had him in four quarters and hanging from a tree. Taking some of the prime cuts with us we headed back to camp and would return in a couple of days better prepared to haul out a large load of venison.

We found when we dressed out the stag that the 100 grain Remington ammo Garry used had blown the animal's lungs out of its mouth. It was something I had never seen before, and was impressed, but doubted that the stag had been. When Garry had fired that shot, everything had gone quiet with all the other stags roaring at that moment shutting down. So it remained for the rest of the trip. It was almost as though a switch had been thrown turning them off. We were sure there was the odd one that would give a single moan, or if we were really really lucky, two moans. But that was the tone for the remainder of our stay.

The rain arrived too, and this country was so steep that it was almost impossible to scale once the soft ground underneath got soaked. Climbing ridges in normal hunting and tramping boots was outright bloody dangerous not to mention attempting to sidle around the faces. Because of this, the stream bed then came in for a fair amount of attention from us, but it produced no results.

The chopper landed dead on time to pick us up and Garry was still grinning like a Cheshire cat when we finally arrived back in Auckland. But then I would have too, if I had shot a nine pointer on my very first Red Deer hunt.

Bring A Danish

It all started with a phone call from Pat Davidson one afternoon. Someone from a large packaging firm in Auckland had been given the job of organising a 'One Day' hunting trip for a Danish representative of their global company, and could I help? Well it seems that organising hunting trips has been my thing for some time now, so I said okay.

I placed an urgent call to Eastern Bay Trappers to secure the chopper for our requirements of that day. After a couple more sessions on the phone it was revealed that this hunter from Denmark, called Henning, was experienced, wore a size eight boot and had a 36" chest. So I was asking myself what does this big wig rooster expect? I thought it best to cover all angles from walking the guts out of him down to having one tied to a fence post somewhere for him to stalk and shoot.

But none of these questions was going to be answered until 5pm on the evening before the lightning trip. I was to meet him in Hamilton so arrived a little early at the motel, only to discover they showed soft porn videos on the room's TV in the afternoons (name of the motel withheld).

I waited around and Henning finally wandered in at the appointed hour with a six pack under his arm. It was DB, but I didn't say anything as it's the thought that counts. He looked like the twin brother of a chap I knew at the range but, all the same, I took an instant liking to him. Within about 10 minutes I had heard his life story and found his English to be very good except that I was now answering to the name Cleef. I corrected him a few times but soon gave up as it didn't really matter.

I told him there would be no guarantees of him shooting a deer and that what we did and where we went would be very dependent on the weather of the day.

'Okay, I understand,' were his favourite words for the next 24 hours.

This guy was really keen so I rang his room at 4am to get him out of bed and he appeared in my doorway not five minutes later complete with his continental brekky tray. Now Henning had a big voice and at 4am in the stillness of the morning it sounded even bigger so I was keen to vacate the room before the management arrived with complaints from the neighbours.

Derek was to have the chopper all warmed up and ready to go at 7am, and so he had, but as usual, there was always a cuppa to be had first. Kate, Derek's better half, did not get her sleep-in that Saturday morning once Henning hit the kitchen with his booming voice. The weather had deteriorated the closer we got to Murupara so we had to go with Plan F. This plan was for us to be dropped off at Wakeman's Clearing, which is a sort of lazy bastard's block. But during the week nine deer had been spotted out in the grass by Joe, the caretaker and watchdog for Eastern Bay Trappers.

The weather was definitely unsuitable but it was about our only option. On our way to the block a spiker was spotted on a slipface and Derek turned the machine about to give Henning a good look at it. The spiker obliged by posing for Henning's video camera before heading off for safer ground, still being pursued by the chopper.

We were put down on the summit, almost landing on two startled deer as we did so, and with just day packs and rifles it took only moments to jump out and let Derek get airborne again. I led the way down to Albert's Hut where we would leave our spare dry gear and lunch — I did say it was the lazy bastard's block.

A hasty scout-around confirmed that the two startled deer had, as expected, cleared out. We could still hear the machine thundering down the valley for a minute or two before its rumblings finally died away leaving the two of us on top of that mountain standing in the pissing rain.

I had loaned Henning a camouflage swanni with a hood and he was wrapped in it like a small child in a sweet shop and I was having my doubts as to whether I was going to be getting it back. Working from the summit we gave the place a good going over but to no avail, despite there being plenty of fresh sign about. Even the wild sheep, which abound on the property, were making themselves scarce.

We returned to Albert's Hut at about 1.30pm which gave us a chance to get into some dry gear and have a bite to eat. Joe also arrived at the hut shortly afterward, asking us how we were getting on. The tinnies were getting a bit low by the time Derek arrived back in the machine at 3pm to hear of our lack of success. So he promptly whipped the doors off the side of the chopper and propped Henning up in the front seat. He then pushed a rifle into Henning's hands and vanished up into the mist and gloom. Now this is a particular activity which I have frowned upon over many years. So why was I standing in the doorway of the hut feeling as envious as hell?

They returned some time later but the exercise had proved to be fruitless even though six or seven deer had been seen and Henning had had a couple of chances which seemed to more than satisfy him. With the chopper doors replaced we piled in and headed for home. Another four deer were seen on the way out and Henning merely shot them with his video camera. He had begun the day with a big beaming smile on his face and it only seemed to get broader as the day went on.

Back in Murupara anything that walked, talked or even moved had that video camera poked at it and all of the people within sight were lined up and filmed while he muttered into the mic in his own tongue. During the trip back he expressed a keenness to see any sets of antlers that I might possess so I made a short detour home to show him my collection, the best of which is only average, but to quote Henning they were, 'totally amazing.'

He was very pleased to meet my wife and I was treated to the same honour when we finally reached the Hyatt Kingsgate Hotel around 10pm. Henning disappeared at a great rate of knots when I pulled to a stop at the hotel's entrance only to reappear a minute or two later with his wife to whom I was introduced with obvious enthusiasm. I was virtually forced to march into the hotel's lounge with its plush deep carpet to 'Come and have a beer, Cleef.'

Henning, it turned out, was one of a tour party of 28 Danes and the whole bloody lot of them were waiting there in the lounge to meet me in my hunting boots, grubby jersey and shorts together with a large patch of dried blood on one bare leg where I had knocked myself climbing over a windfall in the bush.

The reception I received from the hotel staff does not bear a mention except to say I thought the waitress was going to pour my glass of beer over me. I was bloody pleased to get out of the place I can tell you. Finally on my way home and after a very long day, perhaps my most vivid memory, and enduring question that remains, was: Why did all those 27 Danes have to feel, squeeze and examine my legs in the lounge of the Hyatt Kingsgate bar?

Of Stags, Ice and Cigarette Butts

The news was all bad for us when we arrived at Eastern Bay Trappers in Murupara. The weather, although fine and clear overhead, was the opposite at the spot where we wanted to go. The only answer was to wait it out for a day and hope for an improvement in the conditions. It worked, but only just.

Visibility from the helicopter as we approached our target area was barely marginal, but we heaved heavy sighs of relief as Derek put the machine down on the chopper pad which lay under a thick blanket of snow. After watching Derek creep away into the mist we got on with the job of ferrying the gear down to the hut, crunching our way through the snow drifts.

Our wares for this occasion included two very important pieces of equipment. The first was an outdoor thermometer, the second, a portable TV brought along to watch the second All Black test against arch rival France.

My companion for this trip was Ian Weggary, and as we both had some holiday time issued, we put it towards this long weekend trip in the Ureweras. Firewood was quite a problem as everything was covered with snow but we managed to scrape enough together to keep the hut warm.

Very little hunting was done that first day after settling in and cooking lunch. Snug in a warm hut with full stomachs there was no incentive to go wandering around the frozen bush, especially when there were two test matches to be watched on TV. The reception was surprisingly great and with the thermometer outside showing minus five we enjoyed the warmth of the cabin with the pot belly doing a fine job.

Sunday's weather was atrocious with a gale blowing in and bringing with it another dusting of snow so that neither of us strayed too far from the hut that day. Monday, however, dawned bright and clear but still windy. Ian went out for a look around his pet spot while I stayed up on the ridge top.

The snow had formed a hard crust of ice and it became very energy sapping trying to crunch one's way through it. It was a noisy exercise too and I can remember thinking that I might as well have a bloody drummer follow me around bashing the thing with every step I took.

Moments later, while crunching and sliding down a steep spur, my idle thoughts were disturbed by a flash of movement off to my right. A quick glance revealed that a stag had moved up a slip face and was now staring straight at me from about 50 metres away. By chance I had very cleverly blundered into a position where the stag had to look directly into the sun to find out what was making all the noise.

I could see his nose working hard as he tried to get a handle on what I could be. It took some moments for me to sort myself out as I tried to disengage the safety with my mittens. I also had a difficult time trying to find the sod in the scope, as the rifle didn't sit so well against all the layers of clothing I was wearing. But finally, everything jelled and there he was, posing between the crosshairs.

He looked big, and so did his rack, but he was no match for the HPBT Noslers that I used these days. Between the time that I fired and reaching the spot where he had dropped he appeared to have shrunk in stature by about a third. He turned out to be average sized with a reasonable 4 x 4 eight points.

The following day I accompanied Ian while he went hunting down what we called 'Rifle Range Creek'. As I was not carrying my rifle I hung back a little and just wandered along while Ian did the hunting. The going was good with little to no snow down in the gully, but there was no deer sign either, and we soon tired of what seemed to be a time wasting exercise so began a climb back towards the top.

After a few minutes of climbing I got a hand signal from Ian that he had spotted something, so decided to hold back until the shooting was over. Ian however seemed to want me to have a look, so I moved up to where he was to get a view, while he took his day pack off and made himself comfortable in the prone position.

Kneeling down behind a tree I got a peek at the target about 80 metres away on a small clay bank. I could not see its head because of the low hanging branches until it obliged by moving further into the clear area and revealing a set of antlers.

Ian hunts with an old .303 workhorse and he put a shot straight into the animal's boiler room putting the stag into flight and running more or less straight at us for about 10 metres before stopping. It stood still for a few seconds and before Ian could get a second shot away collapsed into a heap. The stag proved to be a young one with an uneven 3 x 2 five points. The steep slip face was covered in ice and proved to be a very difficult place to dress out a beast, but we managed finally, and loaded with meat and antlers arrived back at the hut an hour later.

The following two days were all but useless for hunting due to the severe gales and a visibility of only about 10 metres in clouds that were being driven across from the south-west. At last the snow was beginning to melt with the help of the rain and the time was put to good use tidying up, packaging the meat and restocking the firewood shed.

Friday dawned fine and clear and was to be our last look around as Derek was due to arrive and lift us out the following morning. A big effort was made to add more meat to the larder, but other than sight of a few hinds that quickly scattered, there was no more shooting to be done this trip. So the morning of our departure arrived and it was a long hour spent waiting for the sound of Derek's machine.

The hut had been cleaned, the firewood replaced, and there was little to do but sit in the sunlight and try to keep warm. There was a big surprise in store for us when Derek touched down as there, propped in the front seat alongside the pilot, was my old mate, Jim Dewar. He had come through to Rotorua for the weekend with his wife Betty and their grand-children. He had phoned Derek to see what time we were coming out and Derek had suggested that he come along for the ride. So it was a great end to a good few days' hunting and oh yes . . . the All Blacks did towel the Frogs that weekend.

The King Boar

It happened so quickly and was all over in a flash. A hair raising moment in one of my hunting experiences that remains a pinnacle of excitement. It was during the rut and we were hunting the upper reaches of the Ruahuia River, a tributary of the Kahanui.

We were 2.5 hours away from our base camp, situated in the New Zealand Forest Service hut at the forks of the Kahanui and Mohaka rivers, and a further 3.5 hours' walk from the Land Rover. We'd had a fair measure of success on the preceding days and were looking forward to a continuance of this good fortune.

The roar was not being helped by the insistence of exceptionally fine warm weather, but occasionally a stag was to be heard throwing out a lusty challenge, and here and there fresh sign was in evidence. On rounding one of the bends in the river I noticed a movement ahead, and to the left of us, on a shale slip.

I called Peter's attention to it and instantly we threw our rifles to our shoulders. We were aiming at a mob of pigs, 11 in all, comprising five sows and six suckers. The first of the sows was just disappearing into the fern cover at the top of the slip so I brought my scope down and fired at the last sow in the group.

She crumpled and then, for a second, regained her feet, only to go down again as she lost her footing and slid to the bottom. Peter's .270 was but a split second behind my shot and a sucker was added to the bag. Not content, he fired a second time and again another sucker went down. The last four small pigs didn't seem to be able to muster the courage, or the energy, to get over the lip that bordered the top of the slip. Peter turned and beckoned to me.

In full war cry we put down our rifles and scrambled up the shale after the suckers. We were about 15 metres up and almost to the piglets when in sheer desperation and panic they turned and ran headlong in an almighty spinning turning dash straight down past us.

Peter made a grab for one, but in doing so lost his balance and joined them in a flurry of language in a race to the bottom. Only the overwhelming excitement made him overlook all the cuts and bruises he had sustained. On reaching the bottom he was off again, in full pursuit of his little quarry, and by this time the four of them had all split and gone in four different directions. I watched all this while still standing near the top of the slip beginning to wonder how I too was going to descend without taking a tumble.

Moments later Peter was about 100 metres downstream and

hurriedly removing his Swanni. He jumped into the river only to reappear holding a squealing squirming piglet. It was hard from this distance to decide whether he wore a grin on his face from catching the piglet or a grimace from all the cuts and bruises to his rear end. We congratulated each other and then set about cleaning up our kills and tethering our live one so we could pick them up later in the day.

We continued on up the headwaters for another hour and then decided that the ridge to our left looked the best. We pushed on up towards the 1000-metre tops. But the country we began passing through became increasingly steep with sharp deep gullies, and scarred with numerous shale slips that we had to skirt around. The undergrowth was well eaten out of vegetation so visibility was good for open shooting should it present itself. All that was needed was some game, which as it turned out, was not far away.

The quiet serene surroundings were suddenly broken by the outburst of a young stag who was slightly above us. We were about to move off in his direction when his meagre roar was followed by the mighty bellow of a much more mature stag, one that seemed unconcerned and unconvinced by his younger rival. I pointed to where the bellow had come from and we moved off in that direction. Peter was to work his way into a position where he could see if the stag was of trophy value, while I kept hidden and entertained the beast by roaring back a challenge.

A short time later a third stag joined in, and he seemed to me, to be not more than 100 metres away. So I began edging my way toward this new fellow while still keeping Peter's stag on the go. But the stag I was approaching obviously sensed something was wrong and went quiet. I decided to go back to the original target which by this time was encouraging the whole valley to come up for a brawl.

I moved in a little closer, expecting at any moment that Peter would make contact, but I noticed that the stag was now making its way over to the right, still roaring in full voice. I edged my way through the brush closing in to what I thought were only a few metres from him, but oh what a few metres they were. Straight across from me was little more than a stone's throw, but the intervening ravine was an almost vertical 100 metre drop. I now knew why Peter hadn't arrived sooner.

I started to make my way up the side, looking ahead of me for some way to get over to the opposite ridge, but nothing was offering itself, so I pressed on as fast as possible toward the top. The stag, realising I was moving away, increased his volume obviously thinking his opponent had tired and was leaving. This only helped me to further my exertion because, in my mind, I now had him figured as the largest stag in the area with a majestic set of antlers.

I edged around another rocky outcrop and much to my delight saw that, 50 metres ahead, a waterfall brought the ravine to a halt, and formed an access to the other side. I was inching my way up the last of a steep pinch when directly above me and at about 10 metres away I heard a scrambling of feet and a queer muffled grunting noise.

I quickly gained the top, huffing and puffing, and taking one more step, I was caught completely by surprise. I came face to face with the biggest, meanest, most unafraid piece of pork I had ever encountered. He was far too close for comfort, standing only a little further up the bank. His beady eyes and the ever increasingly rapid chomp of his jaws, covered with dripping saliva, sent a prickling of fear up and down my back. It was a feeling I had rarely felt. This guy meant business.

He moved towards me in a short burst until only an arm

length separated us. The hair on his neck stood erect and his whole body quivered with muscle tension as what seemed an uncontrollable rage overtook him. It could have been only seconds, but it seemed like an eternity, as I pushed my rifle forward and looked into the scope, only to see an over large angry eye looking back.

I aimed slightly right of the eye and fired. This huge boar lurched forward, crashing past me to disappear over the edge of the ravine and land at the bottom with a sickening thud. I reloaded in a flash, pushing another round up the spout, but thinking I wasn't likely to need it. With a .303 between the eyes and a fall over that near perpendicular rock face I thought surely he'd be dead. But incredibly, on landing, he picked himself up and took off in full flight up the watercourse. I brought the crosshairs up to bear on him once more and fired. He stumbled, but incredibly again found his feet, only to at last go down and stay down with a third round in his back.

It took 20 minutes of perilous descent to reach him and, now, standing unafraid next to him I knew definitely that he was still the biggest boar I had ever stumbled across. I was in the process of removing his jaw when I heard Peter call out from above. Once he arrived, I recounted the events to him and, after hearing my story, he quipped, 'Rather you than me mate.'

With that, we set out for camp with a 2.5-hour slog ahead of us, but I was more than content with an exciting day of hunting in the Ruahuia.

Pumice Road

As we topped the brow of a hill we saw the Kaimanawa Ranges standing out just a little darker against the night sky and I mentally traced our intended route up to the bush line. It became obvious though that the New Zealand Forestry Service was having a burn-off of the scrub covered areas leading up to where we wanted to enter and we were going to have to walk through them. It was unclear just how many acres were still burning, but it appeared that our particular path was a real hot spot, so we stopped the car for a discussion.

We had filled the petrol tank in Turangi so had plenty of gas if we needed to drive around a bit, but we finally decided that we would get a bit closer before making any decision. We duly drove up to the burn-off and parked the car off to the side of the forestry road with our plan now being to walk the rest of the way. So after a snack we packed up and headed out.

It was a beautiful night with no wind and not too cold as we made our way under a star filled sky with the only sound being the crunch of our boots along the pumice road. It wasn't long before we reached the forestry gate with the caretaker's house not far beyond that. It was fully lit up, throwing light right across the road. My pack weighed only about 25kg, so it wasn't really heavy, but the perspiration was running down my brow as we quietly trod past. If he came to the door there was nowhere for us to hide and I waited for the bark of a dog to sound our discovery.

For the next 200 metres we moved along in silence waiting for a firm hand to be placed on our shoulders, but it never came and we had nothing ahead of us now but a long walk. We picked up the pace with renewed vigour after leaving the house behind feeling very pleased with ourselves. I was the first to hear it however — the distant sound of an engine coming up the road behind us, and when I looked back there was the glow of headlamps lighting up the bend we had just rounded.

On each side of us was a bank of pumice leading up to pines and we dived for them. I lay face down breathing in the scent of the soft earth as a Landrover came slowly along the road. It had a spotlight and my immediate thought was that the care-taker had in fact seen us and now the search was on. It stopped almost directly opposite me and the beam of the spotlight came to rest on my pack and I was sure the steel frame would be shining like a beacon. I tried to bury myself deeper into the ground but it just wouldn't open up. Then I heard some one shout.

'There's one!' The boom of a 12 gauge shot gun followed, splitting the night.

I think I almost wet myself as I waited for the buckshot to hit me. Instead an opossum dropped dead from the tree ahead of me. This was followed by another volley of shots by which time I knew I had not been seen. Then I heard the driver put the vehicle into gear and it continued on slowly up the road with the spot light combing the trees.

My legs felt a little weak as I dropped back down onto the road with my mate waiting for me and we gave them about 10 minutes head start before we started off again somewhat shaken and covered in pumice and pine needles. We walked for an hour, telling stories and jokes and just generally trying to relieve the boredom of a long walk. The burn-off was now behind us but we could still smell the smoke and there even seemed to be a rise in the temperature of the night air.

Suddenly the noise of the Rover set our hearts racing again and we dived for the cover of the pines once more as it returned. This time I went deeper into the trees, finding a small depression and burying myself in it. Their spot light was of a considerable power because once again it dusted over me as I had my head poking out of the hole thinking myself far enough away. I had the fear that my eyes would reflect back just like any prey and if they had a high powered rifle then I was a target easily mistaken for a deer, but the light moved on as did they.

In total, we had to run for cover four times that night. On the last occasion I was forced to push my way through a tight clump of toi toi and ended up with cut and bleeding hands and a particularly stinging laceration to the side of the neck. I'd just about had enough but the bush line was now only about another 20 minutes away. Back on the road my mate stepped into a pot hole and twisted his ankle. He went down with a yelp of pain and I went to a small stream nearby for some cold water to soak his foot. He drank about half of it together with a codine.

I bandaged his ankle and after a rest we staggered on like two dishevelled lost souls finally making the bush line at 2am where we unrolled our sleeping bags for a well earned sleep. That was just the start of this hunting trip and I remember thinking before dozing off that I now knew what it was like to be hunted.

Sika Country

The long awaited day had finally arrived as Don and I made a last minute check of our gear and then rattled down the southern motorway bound for the airfield at Turangi. It was to be a trip away into the Kaweka Range in search of trophy Sika. Taupo was eventually reached around midnight where we got some sleep in the back of the van until morning and then headed off again for Turangi at first light.

We rattled onto the airfield with plenty of time to spare, as the plane coming from Palmerston North wasn't due until mid morning, so the opportunity was taken to have a hearty breakfast. Jim, our pilot, duly arrived at 10.15am and, minutes later, we were airborne and heading out over the Kaimanawa Range toward the Ngaruroro River and the airstrip at the Boyd where we would land. Jim very thoughtfully circled over the Oamaru and our intended hunting area, Mangapapa, before putting down. The memory of that landing still chills my spine. Before Jim left, we reconfirmed the pick up arrangements for the morning of the 20th and then watched the Cessna as it spun around and taxied back down the airstrip before it came roaring back toward us, taking off with only metres to spare.

Shouldering our packs, we crossed over the valley and climbed Te Kaitetara to pick up the track into our block. It was an easy trail and dusk found us setting up camp in a perfect location on the edge of the bush. During the walk in, we had already heard several stags roaring, which sounded promising, because very little other sign was seen. The next morning we left camp at day break where Don was to go hunting in the country to the north east while I wandered off to the south west. My main intention for this part of the hunt was to secure some meat for the pot.

I had crossed over a high ridge and stalked into the Otorehinani headwater by midday without yet having fired a shot. I had put up two spikers, but my reflexes were not quick enough and they quickly disappeared into the next valley. Fortunately, later on I was able to down a hind and secure some meat for the camp. She had a nice pelt so I took that too. An hour later I was slowly making my way toward a stand of pepperwood from which I had heard a roar from a frustrated stag. But, as so often happens, I felt a breath of wind rise at my back and like a magician he ghosted away unseen.

My luck was to change when a short time later I put up a stag out of a gully and downed him with a neck shot. On inspection his head proved to be a seven pointer with a very narrow span and light in the timber. I arrived back at camp to find Don already salting down a skin which he had taken from a spiker. We traded stories and declared that it had been a good start to the trip. That night we lay in our sleeping bags endeavouring to count the number of stags roaring before drifting off to sleep.

Sunday morning and we were once again away from camp at first light with the both of us heading over into the Oamaru and then on to the Te Tane Rangiharakeke stream to establish a fly camp. During the afternoon we heard some shots from the direction of the Waitawhero saddle so decided to stay clear of that area.

We returned to our main base camp late on a Wednesday without firing a shot and spent the greater part of Thursday morning resting around camp. In the afternoon we hunted through an area that Don had previously covered. Several stags were seen but it was impossible to judge their heads so we left them for another day. That night, over a feast of venison stew, we decided to move camp the following morning into the headwaters of the Mangapapa.

So, at 9.30am on the Friday morning, we moved out and, after an exhausting tramp, located a reasonable site in which to pitch a tent. That was about 2.30pm and 45 minutes later Don and I were on the move once more, this time stalking through the best country we had yet seen. Small open gullies abounded, with practically every one of them showing sign of recent habitation. But, as usual, the wind was everywhere but in the right place so only one animal was seen — a hind that Don promptly knocked over with a neat head shot.

Meat was on the menu once again and with only two full days remaining we were moving swiftly in the hopes of obtaining a head worthy of entering in the annual competitions.

The following day we were about 2 hours out from camp when a stag leapt out from practically under our noses. My first shot missed but the second took him behind the shoulder.

The head was unfortunately a scrubby six points but he had a nice pelt, so I took the skin, though I was also disappointed at having to leave most of the meat behind.

Later that morning I heard the sound of a shot from the direction Don had decided to wander off in and hoped that he had scored a good head, but as I later found out, he had missed. The rest of my day was taken with stalking a roaring animal who persisted in moving all over the place and I finally gave up on him in disgust. I did, however, get a hind in my crosshairs but I let her go on her way.

I wandered back into camp about 5pm to find that for a change I was the first to return. I had the billy on the boil by the time Don came in looking like the most bedraggled and dejected hunter I had ever seen. He didn't keep me in suspense for long and it proved to be quite a tale.

He had stalked into the wind all morning, seeing one four-pointer, which he had not bothered with. Shortly after that sighting he spotted a slight movement on the side of a low ridge directly in front of him and not more than 60 metres away. On scoping the spot he found himself looking at the biggest Sika he had ever seen with the most magnificent head. It was unaware of his presence but all he could see of it was this great head and part of the neck with the body being hidden behind a large tree. He put his crosshairs right in the centre of the neck and squeezed off a shot.

Apparently, a sizable chunk of the tree exploded and when the wood chips stopped flying the stag had departed for safer country. He followed the stag's departing trail for about 100 metres before losing it and spent the rest of the day searching in vain for that great beast. Then, just to top it off, on the way back he tumbled down a bank ending up in a creek with some bad bruising to his left shoulder.

So Sunday morning Don remained in camp resting while I went for a walk in the general direction he had taken in search of this mighty stag. But it was a day without success and by noon I had had enough and made my way back to camp. Over a brew Don suggested we pack up and move out through the Harkness Valley into the Ngaruroro and camp there for the night before moving up the valley in the morning.

We struggled out into the Harkness as darkness descended so spent a night in our sleeping bags under the stars as both of us were too tired to bother pitching the tent. Fortunately the skies were clear and after a good night's sleep and a breakfast of neck steaks we felt a lot better, though Don's shoulder was giving him quite a bit of trouble. We walked out onto the airstrip and waited for Jim to arrive, spending the time yarning, and already making plans for our return trip.

Goats, Goats and More Goats

From time to time the Auckland NZDA Branch would get a phone call from a farmer down the line who was having a problem with feral goats eating all his sheep's fodder and wanting some help in dealing to them. On this particular occasion it was an Alan Smith who had a 2500-acre sheep station on the West coast of Waitomo. So a large party of members converged on the property, with 4WDs providing the required transport from the Homestead to Harihari beach. The bach there was to be headquarters for the three days of Anniversary weekend.

The goats had been conspicuous by their absence as we picked our way along the farm track to the bach expecting to see mobs milling on the hills and valleys. So it took most of us by surprise when we pulled up above the bach to finally see the large mobs which now dotted the hills that provided a backdrop to the beach. Out at sea a Japanese Iron Ore tanker was anchored, loading iron sand from neighbouring Tahore Beach.

Lunch was hastily organised and consumed as we all kept an eye on the slopes and planned for a mop up operation on a grand scale. The animals at first were docile and obviously had trouble working out that their time had come. But slowly the message seemed to get through. As shooters trickled back into camp that evening the large tally started to become evident. In all, 350 goats had succumbed to the might of our cannons in just that one afternoon.

Unfortunately this total was reduced to 349 during dinner when one very large white billy goat, which had been stalked and dispatched by quiet Frank in full view of base camp, decided that somehow it should get up and go walk about, much to the amusement of the many hunters. After the evening meal a bunch of hunters who labelled themselves F-Troop took off up a ridge behind camp. One of their number wore only bare feet and, to this writer's amazement, was seen to walk over, on and through scotch thistles with carefree abandon.

Sunday dawned and was more or less a repeat of Saturday's activities. That afternoon it was decided that a concerted drive should be made on one particular herd that could clearly be seen from camp. Either a lack of communication or planning resulted in one particular hunting party having to dive for cover behind a ridge as hot lead started to whistle by over their heads as a second group below them, but hidden by scrub, opened fire on a mob in their direction. Fortunately only goats suffered from the skirmish, but once the shooting was over, one particular member was seen racing down the hill shouting bloody murder at those below.

The large mob of goats had by now retreated from the head of the valley and out onto the bluffs and a sortie was made along the cliffs that dropped down to the beach. At what seemed the highest and steepest point I came to the end of my .308 ammo so took up position with the binoculars to watch the spectacular action taking place. At first I could see only a mere four goats browsing on the cliff-side seeming to think they were impervious to pursuit on the sides of bluffs where no human would dare to venture.

Then a volley of shots rang out and moments later the number of goats had swollen to 24, running and leaping along this almost vertical drop in a vain attempt to escape the thunder that was raining down on them. It is a sight I will never forget as, one by one, they were hit, fell and cart-wheeled the hundreds of metres to crash onto the beach below.

Monday morning and the hunters were out again, but the number of kills were beginning to decline in comparison to the huge figures of the days before. Finally the rear guard, who had stayed behind while the first of the 4WD trips was made to ferry the hunters out, amused themselves by testing their cannons on a lone billy that had the audacity to poke his nose out of the bush a mere 1000 metres away. With remarkable speed, as he obviously had second thoughts, he beat a some-what rapid retreat. So a great weekend was had by all with a confirmed total of 698 goats falling to 14 rifles.

The Roar of 74

It was an early roar, but a memorable one, and as usual we set off in the early hours of Saturday morning. It was 6 April as we all sat crammed into Donga's wagon and in the front were Donga, Longfellow and Brown-eye. Our destination was the Kaimanawas where we each hoped to shoot a reasonable head for the NZDA branch's measuring night.

We had decided amongst ourselves that no 'non trophy animals' would be shot on this trip as we were going to be a little too far out to carry back any quantity of meat. On the trip down we all told, and listened to, stories of deer that had fallen to Donga's mighty cannon and of the women who had fallen and would fall to Brown-eye. While, from Longfellow, there was just the usual amount of hot air.

A slight problem arose in finding the track entrance to the tops and an unscheduled night was spent on the summit of the range beside the only trickle of water for miles. The next day, around 3pm, we reached the targeted camp site where we hoped to spend the week in splendid isolation. A large snow bank just behind the tent ensured ample refrigeration for our supplies and one can of DB which appeared from nowhere.

Actually, refrigeration is rarely needed at 1500 metres but we also discovered that flies keep away from snow. While Donga and Longfellow pitched the tent, Brown-eye went for a walk to 'get a bit of meat'. Ten minutes later a volley of shots meant that he had found something and had probably missed. Sure enough he returned a short while later to sheepishly confirm he had seen three deer grazing and had missed the lot from 200 metres.

Monday dawned cold and clammy with a low cloud cover that did not clear until midday. It turned out that each day was to be the same up until the day we left when, of course, the weather cleared. Longfellow took off along the range for a scout around while Brown-eye and Donga amused themselves by roaring up a four pointer about half a kilometre from camp. Donga was taken in by the stag's big doe eyes at 30 metres and decided that it looked too good to shoot. What a sap.

Instead he used stones and mule drivers' language to convince the stag he was no lady and, when last seen, the animal was 1.5km away and still running. Later that day the itchy trigger finger of Donga was at last to have its way and a runty four pointer was blown to oblivion 300 metres below and 3kms from camp. Then he almost did himself a mischief by insisting on hauling two legs and the back steaks, not to mention his big cannon, all the way back to camp.

It seemed odd, we pointed out, that he should go to all that trouble when earlier he had chased away a stag of similar size almost within sight of camp. Brown-eye had spent the day around a large peak to the south where he saw three deer, one of which had a good head, but then the mist had closed in at the wrong moment. Longfellow saw nothing except the remains of 42 deer which had been recently shot from helicopters.

He was to see a lot more of the same thing during the next few days, mostly in groups of five or six. It was also his turn to cook the evening meal and while the stew 'looked' nice, it tasted of burned curry and became one of those dinners that were long remembered and remarked upon. After that his culinary efforts were confined to breakfasts.

The next two days were spent exploring the country, mostly down by the bush line where an enjoyable time was spent negotiating bluffs and waterfalls. We surprised some young deer, and others not so young, by attempting to photograph them with standard camera lenses while looking for that elusive trophy head. Certainly there was no shortage of runty heads sporting four or five points.

Donga again came true to form and gunned down a 4 pointer at an estimated 400 metres. Then about half a kilometre further on he came upon a small valley in which there were five hinds and a similar number of young ones which he assumed must belong to some buck. Giving a loud roar he was surprised to see a large stag with 9 points erupt from the bush within 100 metres. One shot secured him his trophy. Naturally Brown-eye and Longfellow were a bit jealous and the blowflies were bloody delighted.

Thursday was another cold cloudy day and in order to pass the time a guided tour of Donga's defunct trophies was organised. He described each shot at length and in great detail, telling us of how big two four pointers had looked . . . until dead. On the way back, the fifth live deer of the day was spotted at a very long range. Urged by Donga, Longfellow loosed off a few rounds at which the deer trotted daintily away, grabbing the odd mouthful of grass between shots.

Donga shouted encouragement as dust flew from near misses and proclaimed that if a hit was made the whole of Auckland would be made aware of the type of head that Longfellow considered a trophy.

Friday was the first day of Easter and Donga spent it cleaning his trophy and shooing flies out of its brain cavity, a spot they all seemed to enjoy. After that he cleaned himself up in a handy stag wallow, and rolled naked in the snow to dry off. Brown-eye and Longfellow climbed a mountain, seeing a further six deer in the process, some of which were at least 3kms away and only visible through binoculars.

Some time was spent discussing the possibility of getting to a rather nice stag but it was decided that the gorge between us and it would enforce a cold night out if attempted. The sight of numerous trampers on the far side of the river valley prompted a quick decision to retreat to the lowlands that night and, after a hurried pack up, we were on our way by 4.30pm. Longfellow was feeling a bit worn out after the day's activities and tended to lag behind on the steep pinches, so Donga blew his whistle at appropriate moments and in army language urged the straggler on.

The river was reached in darkness and with the handy campsites all being filled we set off down river cursing the cold water and slippery boulders. But a most enjoyable evening was later had before a roaring fire in an old camp site where a fly was set up. By 9am the next day we had counted 48 trampers going up the valley and several more came past later. Our return trip took a further two days and included a meeting with a group of nine trampers on top of the first range.

They had no water at all and despite descriptions of how to find water, they evidently could not understand that water was found in valleys and not on top of mountains. That party seemed so inexperienced that a search was later made for them and a billy of water delivered so that they could eat some of their dehydrated food. It took a rough 3-km march to find them in cold conditions. Some people obviously consider exposed mountain tops a great place for picnics.

The Bush Guru

To any onlooker we would have made a comical sight as we clip clopped along that seemingly endless pumice road, under bulging packs, on our way towards our favourite hunting patch. They would have been staggered by the diminutive apparition of a little bloke with a huge pack, wearing a bright orange hat, seemingly on his own, flogging it down a dust road, scores of miles from even remote backwoods civilisation.

My only companion on this trip was my 11-year-old son whose pack bore the combined weight of our two sleeping bags and precious little else. I could be found 60 or more strides to the rear, puffing under the remainder of the provisions and equipment that would be required on this three-day outing. My thoughts wandered back to a time, only a couple of years previous, when a man could easily drive the length of this road, replacing the fresh deer sign with the tread of his 640 x 13 tyres.

Things had certainly changed in a hurry. The road was no longer maintained, except by a few who did only what was necessary to navigate their 4x4 buggies over or around the latest washout. Rounding a bend on a slight downgrade I found that the youngster had come to a halt before a narrow gutted bridge that spanned a small tributary of the stream that the road had been following ever since we left the car.

A few years back the bridge had had a chainsaw put through it by a commercial hunter who thought it a great idea to discourage as many as possible from competing with him for a pack full of venison. Luckily, about six months after that, a group of surveyors had winched the mutilated ends back up and made the necessary repairs.

Over the bridge and another 15 minutes further on had us at the spot where we were to leave the road and scramble for almost an hour up a tiny creek to our campsite. By now the little fellow was content to bring up the rear and benefit from all the better tracks, short cuts and crossings Dad had formed or found during his countless trips up and down this valley. The last little pinch of a climb around a waterfall brought us into a small clearing that was our campsite.

Slipping us both out of our packs, my first job was to check out the gear that had been labouriously tramped in and stowed over the years by my mate and myself. It was unfortunate that two years ago he had developed a rampant kidney complaint and, after all that time, was still waiting for a transplant operation. I knew how much he missed coming in to this spot because I could imagine how I would feel if it were me.

A quick rummage found the axe, shovel, kettle, kerosene

lamp, frying pan and sundry other items all cleverly stowed safely out of sight from any passerby. I erected the tent while the 'up and comer' demonstrated his ability at lighting a fire and making a brew. The camp was organised between sips of tea with our thoughts now drifting towards the forested slopes which surrounded our base. After tucking into a hastily prepared meal we took off for an afternoon stalk.

Fifty metres in from the bush edge we were confronted by a scattering of fresh deer sign which was quickly pointed out by my gum chewing companion with silent hand signals and lots of pointing. I knew very well that immediately ahead of us lay a small hanging basin, which although ideal deer country, had for the last few years received very little attention from the Reds.

Making a sharp left turn we climbed the small ridge which would swing us up and around to a position where we could get an elevated view of the basin floor. A few short minutes later and we stood gazing down into the large clearing, and after a silent pause, while we studied every nook and cranny for a sign of movement, we turned to continue on along the ridge. I had hardly taken two steps before the familiar crash of a Red in panic stricken flight erupted from only a few metres away but on the opposite side of a spur.

We moved forward hastily and I instinctively groped for the rifle bolt as I slung the weapon from my shoulder into my hands. The scope showed two creamy grey Red-deer back-ends flitting away through thick bush on the northern face of the spur. Quickly telling the youngster to sit down and wait, I took off in the direction of the departing animals hoping for a second chance.

Not a bad start to the weekend I thought as I slipped over the side of the ridge. I followed their tracks for about 15 minutes before I gave up, knowing full well that the boy would be starting to dislike having to wait on his own and that there would be other opportunities around the corner.

The weather had been fine and clear all along, but it was now showing signs of closing in as we prepared to turn in for the night, and only moments after snuffing out the kerosene lamp, heavy drops of rain began hammering on the roof of our nylon shelter. But the morning dawned bright and clear again, though a strong breeze could be heard stirring the tree tops above us.

After a bacon and egg breakfast we prepared a cut lunch and put it into a day pack and the two hopefuls once again strode off into the bush. The whole morning was spent in a fruit-less search, as with the young chap in tow, I had decided on tackling the easier portions of this block and thereby bypassing some more productive patches.

After stepping out into a small clear basin I decided that, with it now being 1.15pm, it was time to lighten the boy's pack of our day's provisions. A sheltered bench was selected for this purpose that offered a splendid, almost unobstructed view of the secluded clearing that followed the trickle of a stream for about 100 metres or so. The meal was consumed and we sprawled out in the grass using one hand as a pillow and the other to swat at the blow flies that had crashed the party.

With a full gut we contented ourselves by stretching out and gazing up into the clear blue sky, broken only occasionally by the undercarriage of a native pigeon as he, or she, moved about looking for greener pastures. My immediate thoughts of stubbing out my ciggy were interrupted when a small hand began tugging at my foot and a little somewhat urgent voice whispered, 'I can see a deer Dad.'

Inwardly amused, I slowly sat up to see the boy on his hands and knees at my feet with wide eyes and pointing down into the gulley to my right. Craning my neck in that direction I squinted to try and see what he was pointing at when, 'Cheeses Priced', I muttered.

There was not one flamin' deer but three, all walking in a line along a well defined track on the opposite side of the clearing. Signalling with one hand for the lad to get behind me, I grabbed my rifle with the other, all the while keeping a 'weather eye' on the approaching animals, two of which were hinds and the third, a spiker.

Rising on one knee I decided to concentrate my attention on the latter. I bagged him with one easy shot and his two female companions burst into full flight only to stop before entering the bush to look back toward the scene of commotion with frightened eyes and wildly twitching ears. After they had faded into the bush I was asked why I hadn't shot them as well because they had given me plenty of time to do so. I explained that one deer was all we had come for and one deer was all we were taking.

A short scramble across the gulley brought us over to the kill where the two woody spikes seemed of considerable interest to one in our party, and after much long-winded pleading I was persuaded to take the head home, probably to show off to the local mob of kids. After the customary ritual of removing all of the unwanted and weighty parts of the animal my unloaded rifle was given to the care of the newly converted bush guru and I lead the way back to camp.

The remainder of the day involved skinning and boning out the carcass in preparation for the following day's trek out to the car. The evening meal was consumed while sitting inside the tent doorway as a drizzling rain had set in and appeared to be staying. A pile of dry firewood was sorted and placed under a plastic sheet for tomorrow's breakfast.

The following morning we awoke to a damp mist which had settled over the whole area and guaranteed a wet trip downstream through the soaking scrub. Breakfast was prepared and eaten in record time and after a tidy up around camp we set off for the car.

A Ford Falcon is a beautiful sight after four hours under a 35kg pack, and a stroll down to the nearby stream was rewarded with a can of the local brew which had been hiding there since three days earlier waiting to celebrate this wonderful occasion.

A Day in the Sun

It was in 1978, I think, if my memory serves me right, that I had my last trip into the Woodhill forest hunting the Fallow Deer. In fact I had given away all hope of ever striking the ballot again as year upon year of entering this lottery had passed with no result. But this year, to fool the system, my mate Jim had put in for a permit and included my name on the sheet.

Now I had heard all the yarns about how what used to be only two hunting blocks had mushroomed into seven, and how you got your own personal little map, tags and all the other little bits of crap you were supposed to cart around during the day. Also only bucks were to be shot and if you were to tip over a doe then the sky would fall in on you.

Well something must have hemorrhaged in the system because that evil little machine spat out Sunday 23 September, Block 6, with Jim's name on it and I was overjoyed at the prospect of once again entering Woodhill.

Well the two weeks leading up to our big day were extremely wet and wild and it looked like our luck at striking the ballot was going to be crapped on by the rain gods. I remember sitting in the pouring rain on the Terraces at Eden Park waiting to watch the 'A Team' deal to Otago on the afternoon before our Woodhill date, when 10 minutes before kick-off the sky cleared, and it stayed that way.

So, Sunday morning, shortly after daybreak, Jim pulled up the reins on his Pajero at the forestry gate that separated us from civilisation and our hunting ground. It was windy and cloudy but at least it was dry. There was quite a walk to reach our Block 6, and along the way Jim and I could look across to our right at a lake which was a spot in years gone by where we had nailed three deer. That had been our very first trip into Woodhill and we had taken off for home before 9am that morning with our bounty.

Things sure had changed since then. Everywhere on the side of the road now were little signs that virtually read, 'Keep going sucker, you're not there yet.' But I was becoming impressed because I am one of those blokes who appreciates a bit of organisation. Now I reckoned these signs and all that 'bumpf' I was carrying in my pockets must have taken a fair bit of organising. In time, we came across one of the little green signs which signalled the start of our block and, from there on, the day went very pleasantly for the both of us.

So we parted company and began our hunting. Eventually I was to find Jim in one of the little no exit roads that abounded in the pine plantation. To that stage neither of us could report anything exciting other than having seen a healthy amount of fresh sign about. Then after having morning tea together we separated once more.

There were to be only two moments of excitement that day. One when I breasted the top of a knoll in time to see a little grey bum disappear over the next knob some 20 metres ahead of me. The other was when I stepped out onto the main road, slung my rifle over my shoulder and turned to see a deer tippy toeing off the road a stone's throw away. It was a doe, but no matter, it was just a thrill to happen upon a deer like that anyway.

I wandered over to where she had disappeared and found a patch of pig rooting so fresh that the only thing missing was a pig standing in the middle of it. So the bush was nice to hunt, the going gentle and easy, and underfoot was pleasantly quiet on all those pine needles. There is no doubt in my mind that the Woodhill Fallow Deer Management Committee has done and is doing a great job. I would like to express my appreciation at their efforts. I just hope their ballot machine looks kindly upon me next year.

Southern Comfort

The planning for this major trip had started months earlier. It had to when the undertaking was a weekend hunt in Fiordland with four keen Auckland hunters having to get themselves down to Te Anau and back again in one piece. We had been given dibs on the Lake Shirley-Caswell Sound block. The weather had been fine for days in advance, but on the day we landed, down came the rain. It was estimated that over 500mm had fallen in the preceding nine days and we reckoned that even the Blue Mountain ducks looked dejected.

Now I had been in this block once before, but it had been years ago. I'd had a good trip. On that occasion we saw a lot of Wapiti with many nice looking bulls, so with these pleasant memories, I had planned the trip with a growing feeling of excitement. After a few weeks of planning, everything began falling into place with plane bookings, food and gear lists, water proofing of boots, tents and parkas all attended to. The garage was starting to look like the front line for a major command post.

It was all going so well, and then the first bomb dropped. A letter arrived from the Parks Board informing us that there would be no air drops into the central Wapiti Blocks.

'How in the hell are we going to get all our gear into the base camp?' I thought. It was a gloomy proposition and the thought of carrying a 40kg pack plus a rifle through bogs and rivers and steep faces covered in a tangle of thick matted bush was almost too much to contemplate.

It was a problem left for later, and not for me alone, so over the next few weeks and after many discussions with my hunting mates I started rethinking all our food and gear lists. From my earlier trip I knew it would take approximately two days of solid tramping to reach the chosen base camp at Waterfall Creek. On that occasion though, I had been carrying only a pack of under 20kg and the weather had been brilliant.

The final plans were made the weekend before we left with me repacking my gear three times. We set off from Auckland for the far south with our packs all around the 40kg mark and me wondering how my shoulders and skinny legs were going to stand up to the punishment they were about to endure.

Everything went to plan as we arrived in Te Anau on schedule where we were met at the Manapouri airstrip by Don who had driven down in his Land Rover as pre-arranged. He had also booked us in at a local camp ground and purchased some extra food which we would be leaving behind us at the Glaisnock Hut. Our spirits were high as we looked across the broad sweep of the lake into the misty canyons of Fiordland, thinking of those huge Wapiti bulls roaming around. That seemed to take my mind off the march needed to get at them.

More bad news was to follow, however, as I remarked on the high level of the lake as we went for a drive along the waterfront and past the jetty where the float plane was moored. The petrol pump on this jetty had only the top 20cm poking above the water with the jetty itself completely submerged. In fact, the water level almost seemed to be lapping at the road. One of the local shop owners told us it had been the wettest recorded period in living memory.

Now all hunters are obliged to attend a briefing held by the Parks Board on the Saturday evening where Search and Rescue, radio procedure, transportation, food lists, do's and don'ts are all discussed before one is handed a permit. The weather forecast was not looking good. In fact, it was looking very bad with the float plane pilot warning that we may not be able to fly the next day. But we were to be packed and ready at day break just in case.

Rain had fallen all night, and continued to fall, as we picked up our packs and headed off at a brisk walk towards the lake edge by the tourist office some few hundred metres up the road. As the lake was six metres above its normal level the float plane could not use any of the normal facilities, so sat bobbing against the grass verge by the roadside.

There were two other parties of hunters and trampers ahead of us and they were lucky enough to take off while we stood on the shore watching them disappear into the thickening murk. Approximately 30 minutes later the plane returned and taxied to the edge and up to our bunch of sorry looking hunters sitting miserably in the rain.

'Bertie,' yelled the pilot to his shoreside office worker. 'I can't make the pass again. I can only do a lakeside run, but we have to go now.'

Luckily for us we had one of the lake blocks and this would have been our drop anyway, so we piled on board while other parties that had turned up started to drift away, leaving us feeling very fortunate. As it turned out, those West Coast Blocks were shut for a week. We sat in the plane, about 30 metres above the surface, but it was still like flying through cotton wool and the pilot told us that when he got back it would be the end of any further trips for that day.

He turned the plane up the northern reaches and flew between towering bushwalls and vertical cliffs – it was one hell of a sight. We finally dipped down and touched the lake, taxiing up to what was normally the Glaisnock Beach, only to find that the valley floor was now three metres under water with the tree tops creating a barrier to any solid ground.

I stood on the plane's floats and was about to jump in and swim when a boat emerged from between the branches. A man was paddling out to the plane yelling for us to get our gear on board and he would take us up to the hut. It was such a welcome sight and we thanked our pilot before being paddled back through the trees to the Parks Board Hut. Without the boat we would have had to swim about 200 metres with all our gear through a tangle of bush until striking high ground. Even so, we still had to wade a fair distance before reaching the hut door. We entered soaked.

The party with the boat had a fire going and upon our entrance made comments that are not suitable to print. Don suggested that perhaps we should keep going as we were now thoroughly wet anyway and sooner or later the Tawawera tourist boat would arrive carrying another bunch of shooters which would have this place bulging at the seams.

The grim faces in the cabin pretty much made my mind up

for me so I said, 'Okay, we'll keep going.'

The hut occupants looked astonished at our decision saying that we'd never get across the Henderson Burn.

'I know,' I replied. 'But we will get right up to its face and have a good half day start on any of you buggars coming through behind us.'

The Glainsnock Valley normally has six blocks which means six parties of hunters. Also some of the West Coast Block parties traverse through and over the top which means as many as eight parties could be tramping into the Upper Glaisnock en route. So it made our decision to continue on even easier because we would be the first to enter the Pass.

I've never experienced monsoon rain but as we opened the hut door that's what it felt like and we stepped off the deck into knee deep water. With a final call from within of 'You bastards must be crazy,' we were bid farewell and good luck.

What should have been a two day journey turned into five with us camping in thick bog night after night. Our tents took a real hammering and cooking was a problem as we huddled under the tent flies relying on soups and dehydrated meals for sustenance. But finally four very tired and wretched hunters made the base camp. Everything was saturated but, undaunted, we set about getting a camp fire going with billy poles and firewood. A properly cooked hot meal was most welcome.

The weather was still bad and it had also turned cold, making things even more miserable than before. But having knowledge of the area, and hence an advantage over my colleagues, I was the first to mix it up with the local beasts. I had been crawling through bog for about an hour when I found myself amongst a mob. The bull was big in body with 11 points, but they were small and unremarkable. He had seven cows with him so when I stood up right in the middle of them there was this almighty stampede for cover.

Thinking I had some time on my hands before again meeting up with any prospects I lit a ciggy and stood contentedly puffing away. After about five minutes I saw a young bull step into the boggy clearing and begin walking straight toward me. As he got closer I saw his nostrils flare out as he caught onto my scent, or the cigarette, or both, so I yelled, 'Gidday mate, how the hell are ya?' His ears flicked and I raised my rifle to have a look at him through the scope. 'BANG!' I yelled and this time he was off and running.

After several days our Wapiti count was growing but no one had scored a nice big bull. Dennis and I decided to use a look-out point about 300 metres above the valley floor on a steep face some 45 minutes' climb from base camp. We could always count on seeing around 20 Wapiti from there, and yet we still met with no success for the trophy cabinet.

Dennis was always the first to stir in the mornings and busy himself around camp. So I was awoken on this particular morning with him banging on a tin plate saying, 'Get up you lazy bums, there's a cup of tea ready and it's a nice day.' It was too, the first in nine days of rain.

Later I went off to the lookout again, this time with Doug in tow, and then climbed a further 300 metres to the glacial tarn. The view from this elevated position is absolutely spectacular. The huge glacial valley walls rise many hundreds of metres and in the distance Mounts Tutko and Madeline can be seen climbing up to 3000 metres.

Our binoculars had picked out several mobs of Wapiti sunning themselves out in the clearings after having, like us, endured endless days of persistent rain. Their yellow coats stood out like beacons in the crystal clear atmosphere. Now Doug is nearly 50 years old but he's a determined rugged buggar and as tough as nails. The climb up the 600 metres rock face had taken us nearly three hours, with rest stops along the way, and as we sat looking out at this magnificent scenery I could see the grin on his face.

'Totally worth it,' I remarked.

'Hell yeah.'

Years ago I had spotted a big bull on a terrace from this exact spot and it had taken three days of careful planning and stalking to nail him. Now three years later I was on the spot again looking to repeat my success. There was a large bull below us but his head was small, though his brow tines must have measured a good half metre. He was one Doug had spotted a couple of days earlier.

I was panning across the valley with the binoculars when a cow barked and then dead silence – then another bark. She was nowhere to be seen but obviously she was looking at us. I carried on panning, now down at the terrace, and had the distinct feeling of being watched. I turned slightly and there, 70 metres away, standing side on, was a magnificent Wapiti bull. He was huge with his large antlers creating a frame around Mount Tutuko in the background. Without taking my gaze from him I gently nudged Doug in the ribs, together with a quiet 'There!' from between tight lips. Doug who had been casting his gaze toward the Glaisnock turned without seeing the bull and went to pick up his camera.

'Rifle!' I urged.

Maybe he hadn't heard because he continued to fiddle with the (delete expletive) camera. So, this time a bit more hysterical, I muttered, 'Rifle, rifle!'

The bull hadn't moved a muscle yet and when Doug finally caught on and saw the thing I had to nudge him in the ribs again to keep him from rising. The .303 did a full circle as he brought it around and pointed the muzzle in the general direction of the bull. I think I had already stopped breathing for sometime as I waited for him to pull the trigger.

The shot hit the bull low in the lungs and I saw a splash of blood appear through the binoculars. The animal leapt into the air, lunging forward and down a huge rock face. Dropping the glasses I picked up my Mannlicher, loaded and set the trigger all in one movement while covering the ground between us and where the bull had disappeared.

I leapt down through some boulders and slid to a halt peering over the steep rock face and spotted the bull about 300 metres below and almost out of sight. His huge body appeared between two giant rocks as I lined him up and touched off my hair trigger. He went down and it was all over.

The Fiordland country is very deceptive and it took 45 minutes to get down to him. What a beast, his body was 2.5 metres long with his height at the shoulder nearly 1.5 metres and his antlers were a prize. We both stood looking down at him with some remorse that we had killed such a beautiful animal, but in the end that is deerstalking.

Two hours later we had him skinned and bagged and, while Doug set off back for camp, I climbed back up to the lookout. The day was still fine but it was beginning to turn cold so I put on my warm gear and then set about scanning with the glasses again. Immediately I saw a bull sheltering from the cold wind now blowing up the valley. It was too late to get up and across to where he was, though at first I contemplated taking off after him, but that would mean spending a night out at 1300 metres. Not a pleasant thought as the temperature had dropped considerably and I could see a line of cloud that was making its way in.

Back at base camp the fire was roaring and there was a hot

brew waiting. Dennis said he had spotted a bull and cows feeding above the ribbonwood and was going to go and have a closer look tomorrow. I was going to return to the lookout and watch the terrace. As the fire burned low and we turned in for the night, two resident Wekas moved in and cleaned our plates and mugs with a lot of noise.

The next morning was bitterly cold and I bid good luck to Dennis as he set off down the valley. I left camp and once again started the climb up the huge rock face picking my way through bog and over boulders. It's a fun place where on an almost sheer face at 600 metres you can sink up to your waist in black sphagnum bog. It got colder as I climbed higher and upon reaching the first of the lookouts it started to snow. At the second lookout the wind was cutting through my clothing like razorblades. I had all my gear on and I was still shivering. As the snow eased I climbed higher toward the terrace and the main ridge overlooking Kakapo Creek. But my luck had run out, there was no sign of the bull I had seen yesterday and I was not going to see him again.

I rested in the shelter of a rock face and noticed that the daylight was going very quickly. I was at 1300 metres and about two hours' march from camp with a steep and dangerous face to descend. I was half frozen and had only about one hour of light left and cursed myself for being too engrossed in trying to find that bull. I walked into camp at 7.30pm in the dark, absolutely frozen, sore and disappointed with the day's result.

Dennis had been lucky and after a four-hour stalk had shot his bull. We had one fine morning left to us which dried out the camp. Stinking clothes were aired, boots were dried and blistered feet patched up. I even managed a wash with a pot of hot water while the two resident Wekas had a ball amongst our gear.

Arthur and Dennis were to leave the following day taking a slow trip down the valley and into the Glaisnock with the heads they would carry out to Te Anau. Doug and I stayed on for a couple more days of hunting with me trying a few areas I had not explored before. After Arthur and Dennis left, the weather deteriorated with high winds driving in a thick mist.

We finally pulled our base camp down, despite the conditions, and reluctantly bid farewell to Waterfall Creek. A few hours later we dropped into the Upper Glaisnock and crossed the river for the last time. The going was all downhill from here as we kept to the right of the valley.

As the weather was still bad and the river was on the rise our thoughts turned to the Henderson Burn. If this was in flood we were going to be in trouble and would be unable to cross it. Normally you only get your boots wet but with 4 hours of rain it will rise to over 2 metres and flow at a swift pace. Luckily we crossed but we could see it was rising fast and another hour would make it impassable.

After two more hours of pushing through sodden bush we reached the hut at the lake edge. The lake level had fallen dramatically from where it had been nearly three weeks previously and there was the beach again. A loud roar from down the lake signalled that the float plane was on time. Two very wet, sodden, smelly, hairy Wapiti hunters were on the first leg home to what we hoped was the dry and warm northern climes.

Black Powder

I'm unsure whether it was the news item in the club newsletter or my mate who owns the gun shop in Howick being the cause of it. But, anyway, he had received a couple of replica Flintlock 70 cal. smoothbore muskets. I must have read the article many times over before thinking, dreaming and then finally taking myself down to the shop for a look at these wondrous replicas of an age gone by.

One had already been sold and as I pawed over the last musket I had visions of Daniel Boone stalking deer in moccasins. It seemed a thing of such beauty and I was hooked. I just had to own this gun. It felt like forever, waiting for Monday to arrive as I returned to the shop with my permit and cash clutched tightly in my hand.

I left carrying my prize, plus a couple of flints and a can of black powder. Unfortunately the round ball moulds hadn't arrived and I had to wait a further five months before they finally turned up. After which I spent an evening casting 70 calibre round balls by the dozen.

Next on the agenda was a trip to the range to try it out. Surrounded by a circle of advisers, cynics and rubber neckers I poured in 70 grains of F.G. and rammed home the 400 grain ball and spit-lubricated patch — all the time trying hard to look professional. Next I primed the pan and took aim at the target which was a 30cm steel disc at 100 metres. Suddenly I found myself alone as everyone had withdrawn to a fair distance.

So the great moment had come. I squeezed the trigger . . . click!! Cheers erupted from the crowd with comments about faulty reloads and crook primers. Later I discovered that I should have been using 4F in the pan. However, undeterred I recocked, aimed, and squeezed again . . . click . . . ssss . . . BOOM! A cloud of smoke swirled around me as I realised it had worked. Mighty cheers erupted this time with the information that I had missed the target and struck the bank about 30cm beneath it. I stoked up again and this time aimed at the top of the disc. It fired first try and through the cloud of smoke I heard a loud ring of lead on steel . . . a hit!

I'm yet to shoot a deer with this beautiful weapon but I've had a lot of fun with it and 70 grains of black powder. If you add one-and-a-quarter ounces of shot it also makes a very good shot gun. A dual purpose rifle. What more could you ask for?

Car Case Creek

Why the hell don't I find another sport, like bowls or darts, instead of this stupid bloody game? This was just one of my more printable thoughts as I waded for the umpteenth time through freezing blasted waters with the hind quarters of the mother of all hinds on my shoulders. The dead weight was doing its best to knock me off my balance and give me a dip in the swollen stream we called 'The Car Case Creek'.

Now Car Case Creek was one of those blocks that come under the umbrella of Eastern Bay Trappers and it got its name from the hut built on its banks. There are no prizes for guessing that the structure began its life as a car case. It's the great Aunt of all huts and sports two bunks, the top one of which is only inches from the ceiling which does not take into account, nor consider, the pot bellies and aging bones of refined gentlemen such as we.

As a consequence I elected to sleep on the floor and let Jim have the lower bunk. This made for very little room at night, but at least the nocturnal de-watering trips were a little easier for the gentlemen who could no longer go the whole night without a bladder appointment. Unfortunately the outside thermometer was touching minus one degree centigrade and it was a mighty battle of wills between the bladder and the extremities.

At one end of this building is a fireplace and woodbin with the odd precarious shelf for standing one's knick knacks on. Needless to say, room of any kind is at a premium in this hut, in fact two is a massive crowd. The one big plus going for it is that it is easy to keep warm and dry.

It was only that morning that Derek had put us down mere yards from the hut. My first impression was that the stream seemed to be running a little high after all the unseasonable November rain. Access to the area is perfectly possible on foot from Pine Milling Road but the chopper allows for a few more luxuries and home comforts to be carted in.

In less than an hour our gear was stored and we had togged ourselves out in our hunting clobber and were heading off to two different points of the compass. I went downstream while Jim took the easier option going upstream. Some hours later I returned to the bivvy and found Jim was back from his hunt and sitting in the sunlight on a beer crate with the grandfather of all grins lighting up his face.

I knew without asking that he had made a score. About two cans of Double Brown later and I had heard the whole story. It seems that he had been sneaking along on the left- bank of the stream and came to a bend. As he rounded it he saw three big cream coloured bums going away from him at a rate of knots.

His first shot missed but turned them towards a bank that they were never ever likely to be able to scale. They came to a milling halt. He restoked the chamber of his .308 Remington 600 and had another pop at them. The second round also missed but seemed to make their minds up for them and they resumed their original course upstream. Just as they were about to disappear he took a bead on the last animal, at that little brown spot just below its tail, and let rip.

Apparently the reaction was spectacular with the beast doing a complete cartwheel before disappearing. Hurrying after them he found the hind down in the stream lying stone dead. The bullet had collected the animal right in the back of the head. He then proceeded to dress out the hind where it lay and with that job completed returned to camp to wait for me.

Now Jim, with his dicky hip, would have been courting disaster had he tried to bring a load of meat back to camp, and besides, that's what was I there for. Mercifully the scene of the action had taken place only about 15 minutes' walk from the camp and, with two quick trips, I had all the meat back and hanging in the safe.

I left Jim to complete the boning out and went off to prepare our evening meal. Jim stepped back into the hut sometime later with his butchering job completed. Our tea for that night was rump steak, veges and chips. While the meal was cooking I began tippling the old dark rum and coke to a stage where the tide was almost reasonably out in both bottles.

Now I usually pride myself as a bit of a cook, but 'sumthin shur wint ronng thit nyte' and we ended up having to eat what amounted to bits of shoe leather. The steak was way the hell overdone and the chips ended up being boiled in oil rather than fried, the noodles turned into a kind of paste but I think the surprise peas and beans came out okay. Anyway Jim seemed too preoccupied laughing at something or other to notice.

The next day, Saturday, was to be my day, or so I thought. I was going to go further a field than I had ever been before on that block, which I did, and yet I returned to camp that night empty handed and feeling like something a dog had discarded. My only reward for all my hunting was to discover a camp site where someone had been poaching. They had left behind a fairly decent cast antler and a double ended deer trap. There had been heaps of deer sign but no sighting of any animals.

That evening was a cold and uncomfortable one as my lilo had sprung a leak and the night was mainly spent lying in my sleeping bag listening to the opposums outside cleaning the evening meal's billies. Sunday then dawned with the sister of all frosts and the stream water was so cold it now became a painful exercise to cross. But off hunting I went although, as it turned out, I may as well have stayed in camp.

Derek was due to lift us out at 10am and we were packed and ready long before then. He arrived shortly after the appointed hour, roaring into sight above us, and in very quick time we were buzzing our way back to civilisation. There was only one real lesson I had learnt that trip, and it was, if Jim ever tried to boot you up the pharter, you needed to get your head well out of the road.

Editors Note:
In his later years this hut was to become Clive's regular haunt and he was given permission to build onto the existing hut. Regular trips were made to local recycling depots for building materials which would eventually include a bath, shower and toilet. He and his hunting mates Jim Dewar and Brian Wilson would eventually create a home away from home that was to become known as Clive's Hut.

Sometimes You Lose

The still morning air was broken by the harsh screech of a Kaka whirling above and the plaintive cry of its mate on one of the neighbouring ridges. I was sitting on the edge of a shale slip overlooking a small flat clearing beside the river below waiting in vain for a glimpse of the big stag I had seen there two days before.

I knew he wouldn't be too far away as I had not disturbed him on that earlier occasion. I was beginning to think though that I had drawn another blank and reached into my pack for another biscuit. These biscuits were something my mate had knocked up a few days before, and apart from being hard and tasteless, they weren't too bad. Certainly he was not going to put Griffins out of business. I had just begun to chomp away when I saw it.

At first I wasn't sure, but then very cautiously, a head appeared. I focused my scope and saw it was a hind, and then another walked into view, and another. All three were feeding and making their way towards the river. Was he there? I thought. He must be. A roar in the distance took my concentration for a moment and when I looked back there he was. Ten points of the most beautifully developed antlers I had seen.

My heart skipped a beat. Would I be able to get a shot? I was about 250 metres from him, but he was standing near the dark shrouded bush edge, and a shot from here was too risky. I inched my way back out of sight and started to edge my way down the scrub line. It seemed to take forever and I chanced poking my head up to take another look. Yes he was still there with about 150 metres now separating us. Just a little closer I thought, wondering if I wasn't pushing my luck.

The wind, or what there was of it, was blowing into my face so I knew that wasn't going to give me away. I moved slowly, trying to eliminate all noise down to a point where the stage was set. Another look out through the scrub showed that all was well with the hinds milling at the water's edge some 30 metres away and the stag sauntering over to them.

At that moment there was another roar from above, yet this hardly seemed to arouse my stag at all. Sunlight was beginning to filter through low cloud as what had started out a grey old day now showed signs of brightening up. I checked everything over one final time and then carefully poked myself into a small gap in the scrub on the edge of the shale.

I zeroed in on him, knowing this was going to be the first big test of my new telescopic sight and brought the crosshairs to sit just behind his front leg. Holding my breath I squeezed and . . . click. I couldn't believe it, a bloody misfire. He must have had sharp ears because they pricked up like antennas as I struggled in the cold to eject the dud shell and load a new round. But, before I could, I suddenly found I was not maintaining my balance and had begun to slide. I turned back to grab at the scrub but it was just out of reach and I now found myself on a slippery ride down towards the river.

My main concern now was to secure myself and my rifle and I dug my heels and free hand into the loose scree looking for support. Luckily I found it in the shape of a small jutting rock and was able to halt my descent. The deer of course were gone, racing across the shingle, heading down stream, and quickly out of sight, barking as they went.

I half slid, half fell, in my effort to get down onto the river-bed safely. The deer were gone and I knew it to be folly to go in after them. Instead, I turned my attention to my dud shell, ejecting it for a look and noticing for the first time that it felt a little light. I gave it a shake to finally realise I had somehow managed to load it without any powder.

Putting it in my pocket I headed up river knowing I could follow a small side tributary that would take me back to the bivvy and a warm brew. Later, as I had kept the misfired round, I mounted it on a board to hang above my work bench as a reminder to the best 10 pointer that ever got away.

Hell and Back

I crawled my way up the ridge on hands and knees, with blood oozing from the cuts in my legs, and the pain in my lower back suggesting I had been hit by a bus. My mind was hazy from lack of sleep, cold and exhaustion as I looked back on the last 24 hours.

My mate and I had left the hut after a light breakfast and headed for a second hut down river. It had been raining all night and although the river was high we thought we could make it. The first river crossing was achieved without any trouble but the second proved harder to negotiate. The water here was a dark muddy colour and the rocks on the river bed were slippery.

The water was moving fast as the rain continued to pelt down and it was very cold, so you had to keep moving before your joints decided to seize. Out in these conditions you don't talk very much but you sure think a lot, and I was thinking, 'What the hell am I doing out here when I could be in a warm hut with a beer.'

I realised we had made the wrong decision and I turned to my mate, who was beginning to look like the drowned rat I felt I was, and said, 'Lets go back, this is bloody stupid.' He nodded and turned right around as obviously the same thought had been on his mind for a while, but perhaps he had not wanted to say anything, and instead had put his trust in my knowledge of the area.

Well we tried to recross the river but it had become impossible and both of us knew the folly of pushing one's luck on a swollen river. 'That's it!' said my mate. 'We'll just have to try and make it to the one down river.'

Now I had travelled between the two huts before, but only along the river bank, and it had required many crossings. But the conditions had been good then and I knew we were not going to be able to reach the hut by that route. High ridges rose on each side of the river and there were some very steep gorges that I was certain we would never get through. The river flowed in a very large curve and I figured that if we headed across a couple of ridges we would find a small tributary stream that ran into this one at the other end of the curve, and that was where the hut would be.

In those days I was fit and never carried a compass or a map. I relied instead on ridge formations and observations to navigate my way around. The only trouble with that reasoning was that when we got onto the first ridge we found that visibility was zero and by this time we had been going six hours. I could feel the pangs of hunger and cursed having eaten only a light breakfast.

In good weather the trip between the two huts normally takes about 3.5 hours. We decided to continue walking until close on dark and if we had not reached the hut would camp out and start early again the next morning. At about 6pm that evening we dropped down a steep ridge and found we had miscalculated direction and were now in the bend of the main river with still two thirds of the way to go.

By this time we were both in poor condition, with the lack of food and hard slog beginning to take their toll. We picked a suitable campsite and my mate began to build a bivvy with fern fronds and branches. I shot and skinned an opossum and managed to start a fire which was a mammoth task as everything was saturated. But I found a spot under a fallen tree where there was some dryness and gathered some moss and leaves together. I hung my swanni above the spot and emptied about 10 rounds of powder into the leaf pile to get the fire going. That night we ate half cooked opossum and slept huddled together under a dripping fern cover.

The next morning in the half light we shook ourselves free of the cramps and aches and decided to head back out the way we had come. The rain had eased a little but even so, the small streams we had crossed the day before had now become major obstacles. The only way of crossing them was by crawling across the trees that had fallen in the night. The weather had been bad and I could not remember when I had seen rain as torrential as this. I have little memory of the journey back. I just followed my mate who seemed to be surviving this ordeal better than I was. I do know that at one time while trying to cross a stream I slipped and fell about 15 metres. My mate dragged me out as I came up for breath. I sat on the edge of the stream and found that when I closed my eyes the cold and pain went away. All I wanted to do was just lie down and go to sleep.

But I was brought quickly back to reality when I heard the voice of my mate loud in my ears. 'You waiting for a bloody bus or something?'

I looked up at his face and his eyes were glazed. There was anger there, but there was a bit of panic too. Christ I thought, I hope I don't look as bad as you and I started to move.

Thirty six hours after we had left the hut we made it back. It was just on dark as we staggered through the long grass over the last 50 metres to the hut door. There was a fire going, a hot billy of tea brewing and the ugly mug of one of our mates grinning back at us.

'Hell,' he said. 'No sooner do you brew a tea and look what the cat drags in. I must have gotten here just after you blokes left. Get into the sack and I'll fix you some tucker. Anyway . . . where ya been?'

The UFO

We had set off at noon on the Thursday in order to take full advantage of the long weekend. On this trip I had my son and his mate and two of my regular hunting buddies with me. We were all packed into the Bedford van, towing a trailer laden with our gear and one 50cc Suzuki mini bike. The 4-hour journey down was uneventful enough and we stopped at our regular haunt, the Tirau off-licence for a feed and a pint. The boys were too young to enter the tavern but were happy enough with a pile of fish and chips from the take-away opposite.

Not wanting to waste too much time we hit the road again hoping to be the first to claim the saddle hut situated deep in the Kaingaroa Forest where the largest pine plantation in the southern hemisphere ended and the native forest began. But a sudden large pothole in the middle of a forestry road put those plans on hold when it stripped the cam belt out from under us and we were unceremoniously brought to a halt.

It was 20kms out to the nearest town of Murupara and the day was getting on, so we realised it was too late to do anything but set up camp next to the road and sort it out in the morning. I was awfully glad for bringing the mini bike on this trip as a 20-km hike through pine forest wasn't what I had planned for the weekend.

I took off after an early morning breakfast and must have looked a sight disappearing down the road on the little machine at full throttle, which with my weight and the bumpy road, was at only about 25km per hour. The chap who owned the garage in Murupara was most obliging, and being a hunter himself, closed up his shop, threw the mini bike on the back of his tow truck and arrived back with me to fix up the van.

We were on the road again in short time and made the hut, relieved to find it stood empty. Once comfortably ensconced, we sorted out some firewood and had a good lunch. The boys were eager to be off as we had seen a lot of bunnies on the way in. They loaded themselves onto the mini bike with their .22 rifles and headed off to explore the vast network of trails and logging roads that offered an abundance of rabbits and hares.

The area had been milled only a few years earlier and the replanted pines were only about a metre tall set amongst the thick tussock that carpeted the hills. Small calibre rifles were not permitted in the area so I told them that if they saw anyone they were to disappear and lie low.

Ian had already disappeared for a stalk and I left Kevin still getting his shit together and headed south along the bush line. I had gone perhaps a couple of kilometres when I came to a gully filled with the broken remnants of felled trees and deep erosion runnels in the pumice soil. It was not a landscape worth traversing, though a large fallen pine, either unwanted or forgotten, spanned the gully giving access to the forest on the other side and to a nice set of ridges that I decided I would come back and hunt tomorrow.

We had been blessed with fine weather and the next day I went back along the tree line and over the felled tree. Making my way across this natural bridge through a tangle of branches I entered the native bush and got onto the first of the ridges and worked my way quietly up to a small plateau. While there was an abundance of sign, it was not all that fresh, and I continued on until I reached a point where the system kicked back in the general direction of the hut. I was making my way down this adjoining ridge when I heard a distant shot. There was only the one boom and it sounded to me like Ian's 30.06.

When I got back to the hut Ian was dressing out a hind. He said he had gone for a walk up the track behind the hut and 10 minutes into the stalk she had stepped out in front of him basically committing suicide. I, on the other hand, had not seen a thing. That night, with full stomachs, we sat outside gathered around a brazier, drinking tinnies and talking a lot of rubbish and some hunting.

It was a beautifully still crystal clear night with a sky you don't get to see living in the city. The heavens were littered with stars and, as we gaffed, Ian pointed up and said, 'What's that?'

Coming towards us was a bright light, about twice as bright as any star.

'Can't be a plane or we'd hear it,' I said.

'Too high maybe?'

'Satellite,' said Ian.

Then as we watched the thing approaching, expecting that it would go over our heads, it executed a right hand turn. Not a slow turn but an immediate ruler-like right angle and went off toward the west.

'Satellites don't do that,' I said.

'Nope. Planes neither.'

'No way.'

We watched as the thing glided away, disappearing behind the dark silhouette of the ranges. About that time my bladder was complaining that I had drunk enough so I wandered over to the edge of the bush to relieve it. I noticed that everything seemed to have gone quiet. It was almost too quiet, as the forest night life had gone completely silent and I was left with the unalienable feeling that something was watching me.

Now I'm not one for ghost stories or spooks, but I can tell you that at that moment a sense of dread gripped me like I had not felt before, and suddenly within the black confines of the bush I felt some sort of presence. Whether it was the beer, or some irrational moment, I don't know, but I finished the task and strolled back to the fire.

'Think I'll turn in,' I said.

The others soon followed suit and there seemed to be some sort of unspoken mutual feeling of retreat as we shut ourselves inside the hut.

The next morning we headed off home and little more was said about the event except that my lad remarked to his mother that we had seen a UFO. I laughed it off but internally I've always wondered just what that bright light in the middle of nowhere was – a silent gliding light that did a turn like no ordinary craft has ever turned.

Tinbum

I should have stayed back in the hut, I thought. It wasn't the incessant light drizzle that was bothering me but the howling wind. It was blowing the trees about so much that I could hear the constant crack and thud of branches falling all around me. But then I had just come over a rise and there protruding from behind a big beech tree was a deer's rump.

Now one of the most common questions I'm asked, especially by novices, is where do you look for deer? Some hunters will say look for them in the high country during hot weather or down in the streams at dusk and dawn, while others will suggest in the basins in spring. Then there are those who will advise the complete reverse. One hunter with whom I have spent a lot of time swears they are to be found in the sheltered or leeward side of the hills on wet and windy days.

His theory is that deer feel the cold just as much as the hunter and will therefore have the sense to stay out of the wind. While I agree this makes a sort of sense it certainly wasn't holding true for the deer I was looking at now on such a particularly atrocious day.

The deer was apparently feeding so I was able to sneak up to within 30 metres of it. I sat down behind a log, put the rifle down and began extracting my camera from a plastic bag. Even with the noise of the wind and falling sticks all around it seemed incredible how thunderous the noise of opening a plastic bag was when so close to a deer. I had yet to extract the thing when the deer decided to swap ends and look my way.

I, of course, froze and the animal resumed its browsing, wandering back and forth across the narrow ridge but gradually working its way over to me. I crouched down and waited and could hear the blood drumming in my ears like a pneumatic hammer. Closer and closer she drew and I could see her coat was ruffled and wet and her big ears were twitching this way and that.

I was in a turmoil of indecision as I struggled with whether to risk spooking her by continuing to try and extract the camera from the infernal plastic bag or to whip the rifle up and shoot her. She was mere metres away munching along with her head down in the grass. She swung left to walk by the log and then stopped, standing no more than an arm's length away with just the log between us.

I leapt to my feet and sprang over the log in a mad impulse to smack her with my hand. She recoiled in terror and such was her fright that her back sagged, her head rose, and her feet began flailing like a windmill. She was in such a panic that her feet shot out from under her and she went down, legs going in all directions until she rolled, sprang up and bolted. Her gazelle-like springs took her out of sight in just a few mighty bounds.

That particular hind was an exception to my hunting buddy's theory which obviously, at best, is a generalisation. Another friend used to pay no attention to likely spots because he had been through them so often and had never seen a deer there that he just gave up hope of ever doing so. I, on the other hand, lived in hope, realising that it would be so much easier carrying a deer from these clearings than from some place further away.

Then one morning, sure enough, a hind and her yearling bounded up a slip. I'm a rotten running shot but, much to my surprise and delight, my first shot brought down the hind, though by the time I had reloaded, the yearling had disappeared into the bush. It is an experience that brings to mind similar situations in which hunters, upon entering a new area they have never hunted before, will shoot a deer almost right by the road. It highlights the fact that one should start hunting right from camp regardless of how infrequent precious sightings of deer may have been in the past. Cast your mind back to the stories other hunters have told you on how they came upon a deer and of how you quietly thought, 'What a tinbum'.

Knowledge of a deer's preferences for certain areas can save one a lot of time and legwork, but it pays not to become too iron-bound on theories. So my advice to those who ask me the question of where to find deer is this: the deer are wherever you find them.

Three for Three

The final arrangements for the weekend hunt were made during the evening of our monthly meeting where Ross, Dave and I decided it was all on. The weather forecast was bad, but when the stags are roaring a little bad weather does not deter us. Dave picked me up at 5am sharp as we had a long way to travel down the southern motorway with him flying his Valiant through the persistent rain. My thoughts raced ahead to our destination where years ago, as a single man, I could leave the old home town at the same hour and be in the bush by daybreak. Today it would take 6 hours of travelling.

It was early afternoon when we arrived at the end of the road. The main ranges looked clear but it didn't look as though it was going to last as a front was moving in from the west. A thick blanket of cotton-wool-looking mist was draped around the summit of a high peak in front of us as the three of us began a 3-hour splash up the main river with our parkas kept handy for when the downpour finally came.

Fortunately the water level was low and after a long continuous struggle up the cold river we arrived at our first hut. No deer had been sighted along the way but we were to find out later that a meat hunter working along the river bed and adjacent slips had shot four during the previous few days.

The hut had been built by the Forest Service and with its wooden floor, concrete fireplace and rubber mattresses was a home away from home. During dinner a hunting party who had been in a side branch of the river arrived at the hut on their way out. They had spent five days fly camping and were soaked to the bone. They had found the stags to be roaring but had also found it difficult to coax any out. However they had shot five from 19 sightings so were pretty pleased with their trip.

The deer that existed in this area were originally an English Park deer release and had never shown any great trophy potential. Their numbers had swelled dramatically but meat hunting and heavy culling had taken its toll on the population reducing it to the advantage of the private hunter. I could remember a time in the 1950s when two hunters on a weekend trip could knock over 20 deer for their skins without too much effort.

The area covers many thousands of acres with ranges going up to 1500 metres. The tops are pure tussock and a hunter could literally walk for days and days. The coming of the chopper hunters has decimated the large mobs of yesterday but thankfully there are still a lot of deer in residence.

Ross made short work of rousing the hut occupants long before dawn on the following morning after stubbing his cold bare toe on an unseen object in the darkness. For his trouble he was offered an assortment of unprintable language from the occupants of the other bunks. Dave, after a quick brew, took off for a scout around up a small creek. Ross and I decided on a full day of hunting, so we packed a sizable amount of provisions to take with us. We bid farewell to the homeward bound party and headed off upstream.

A short distance above the hut put us in the middle of a gorge where I skated off a large greasy boulder into a deep pool. Ross helped retrieve me but I was soaked in freezing water from head to toe. The numbing cold as I stood starkers on a shingled bank wringing out my underwear wasn't helped by Ross's comments.

The decision to carry on was made with some reservation on my part, but we decided the river could become worse and we would get wet anyway. We were now in unfamiliar country though I knew there was a second hut in the area situated up a side creek, though was unsure which one. We hunted for two more hours without luck in the wet bush beside the river. A mixture of bush craft, map reading and a little cunning then put us on top of the second hut. It had been a long shot to wander up this particular tributary but the bet had paid off and at 11am we entered. This hut isn't used as often, as it is right up under the sub alpine scrub and a fair way back.

Like the first hut it was left well stocked before the cullers pulled out, and we were able to get a roaring fire going to dry our wet clothing out. I stood with my back to the fire toasting my whole body in my best nudist camper outfit and was reminded of the yarn about an unwary Auckland Girls Tramping Club being surprised by male trampers in the

Waitakere Ranges.

A warm up and hot meal had both of us feeling much better so that our thoughts returned to hunting. The stags were keeping quiet and up until now we hadn't heard one roar. We decided to pick up a leading ridge to the top and then hunt them in the wallows. After 45 minutes of climbing, fresh sign was becoming evident though continual use of the roaring horn didn't bring any replies.

It wasn't until the top was reached and we stopped to exercise the horn once more that we received our first customer. Unknown to us we had climbed to within 100 metres of this stag's wallow. He gave an almighty bellow and charged through the bush towards us. He took us completely by surprise and it was several seconds before we collected our marbles and ducked down behind a log. I roared back at him and he again replied with a further crashing run that was bringing him right to us.

A long silence followed and then suddenly he appeared about 25 metres away, staring intently through the bush in our direction. I could see him clearly through my scope, and the fierce expression in his eyes. I squeezed the trigger on my 7mm.

He was an 8 pointer and a big one, scoring 204 on the Douglas, and made a fine classic style trophy. Ross had also fired, almost at the same time as myself and we were excitedly chattering away while preparing the head when we were brought to silence by another loud bellowing roar from close by.

Ross roared back, as my throat had started to feel somewhat hoarse, and he got into a duel with the beast. The cold wet bush vibrated with the challenges and the excitement became intense as this second stag crashed towards us in a frighteningly angry mood. He gave one further almighty bellow and then fell silent. He gave no answer when Ross roared at him and it was obvious that he was stalking us. We remained frozen still with the dead stag which must have been camouflaging our own scent.

After a long pause Ross moved off up the ridge for about 20 metres and was sneaking over to a dead log when I spotted the stag. It was standing motionless and staring at Ross who was only 10 metres from him. Ross was so intent on reaching his cover position that he was clueless to its proximity and I realised that within a few seconds he was about to come face to face with the animal.

I hoisted my rifle and the stag completely filled the scope. Gently squeezing the trigger for a second time on the Mannlicher, the boom I expected to hear was replaced with a loud metallic click. In all the excitement I had failed to reload the rifle and had only reset the trigger. The sound of the bolt being moved swung the stag around. Ross being now within 10 metres, and the sound of the stag doing his acrobatics almost on top of him, must have nearly been cause for a replacement set of underwear.

The stag, which had a nice trophy head on him, leapt from sight and I cursed myself for my mistake. Two stags within 25 metres was obviously a little too much to ask for and would have to be consigned to the 'ones that got away' yarns. I told Ross what had happened and we continued to dress out and prepare the first head while he mumbled something about novice shooters.

But we were soon back on speaking terms and chatting away when once more we were stirred into action. Another stag gave a loud bellow within 100 metres of us but down on the other side of the ridge. I had a go at replying and he started to come over. With our task completed on our first trophy we hastily packed up and headed straight over to this new animal that was roaring his head off.

On breaking out into the leather leaf I gave a roar which was immediately answered and we could see where he stood. There was a steep slip about 150 metres away and he made a beautiful sight with his head thrown back, roaring at us. Ross shouldered his .308 and made no mistake with one good clean shot and it was all over. It had certainly been a day to remember.

Two hours later this pair of weary hunters arrived back at camp in time for a cuppa of Dave's tea and the welcome warmth of a fire. It was almost dark and the outside temperature had dropped to the 5-degree mark. The next 2 hours were spent in front of the fire drinking hot chocolate and reliving the day's events. Dave found the country that he had selected to hunt quiet, with no deer seen or heard.

The following morning the weather deteriorated and we left camp in a light drizzle. It was bone chillingly cold and the first river crossing was most unpleasant. We emerged from the other end of the gorge with ribald chatter but at least we were through the worst section. After another 45 minutes in the river we reached the turn off. This creek was another branch that lead up and out onto the tussock.

This was new country to me and when it became gorgy we decided to go straight up through the bush to the top of the ridge. It was a steep but welcome climb as the rain had set in and our cold legs and feet warmed up as we scaled the sheer face. At the top of the ridge we gave some tentative roars and were rewarded with two replies. But the stags were on the opposing ridge and that meant going back down into the river again, so we held off, wondering what to do.

Thoughts of a nice warm hut came racing back as we huddled under a thick Mountain Beech tree trying to open a cake of chocolate with stiff frozen fingers. The packaging finally yielded and we consumed the chocolate as three shivering long faced hunters tried to make a decision on their immediate plan of action. Five minutes later and snow began to fall, coating the bush in a thick white blanket that stood still and silent. It began to come down thicker and thicker and the temperature began to drop alarmingly quickly.

We decided to carry on for another 30 minutes along the ridge and then drop straight down into the river which would put us about an hour and a half from camp. We had been prepared for the cold, but all three of us were shaking now with the deteriorating conditions. The snow was dense and visibility had reduced to a few yards. Before leaving the ridge I gave a few roars but received no answers. Ten minutes further on Dave, who was leading, flushed a hind that sprang away into the snow filled bush. Another 5 minutes and another hind, but this one stood peering intently towards us through the canopy of snow. Ross motioned Dave who was preparing to smoke down the hind and pointed to me to give a roar. Dave held off until I had roared and an answer quickly came through the frozen bush.

This stag was about 150 metres in front of us and his hind ghosted away, totally unaware of her good fortune. Another 10 minutes passed as we quietly moved forward through the bush until we were within 50 metres of the stag. The snowing had stopped and the excitement of the last 15 minutes had us all warmed up. Another roar from us brought a fierce reply and the ensuing vocal battle started another stag in the vicinity. As we stalked on ahead, the ridge flattened out to a boggy saddle with its accompanying wallow. The noise of the two stags grew louder as we approached to within metres of them.

Through the beech trees we saw a hind standing motionless,

watching Ross moving forward. I roared at her which started her stag going with a vengeance. He was down off the ridge, but well hidden, while the other fellow had moved away on a blind ridge a further 150 metres down. Another roar from me gave Ross and Dave the chance to move in closer. The noise being made by the two animals in the snow covered bush was exhilarating.

Suddenly a hind sprang into view just metres ahead and I gave a loud roar at her. With this the stag jumped out of some cover behind her and Dave raised his .243 and fired as he raced across in front of us. It was a well placed shot and he dropped motionless into the snow. He was an 8 pointer, very even and of a good size.

So now three very weary, wet and cold hunters clawed their way out of the river onto the terrace and made it back to the hut by 5pm. The head waters in this area are very steep and hunters are constantly soaked through travelling in fast flowing rivers and creeks. Bad weather is just a constant reminder of the dangers of exposure, especially where the temperature can drop 30 degrees in an hour.

We were back at camp and pleased to be there too. During the night a gale force wind shook the hut and heavy rain forced the river up quickly. No one stirred until 9am the following morning and we just lay in our sleeping bags while the hut shook and the rain came down.

Ross and I went out after lunch and climbed straight to the top of a 1200-metre peak. But the wind made hunting impossible. We did walk into a nice stag but he sprang away having seen us before we saw him. By now the wind was back to its gale force ferocity and, fully protected as we were in our clothing, the chill still seemed to cut through like razor blades.

The next morning and the river had returned to more normal levels but it was still bitterly cold. We packed up and headed off down the river track. Driving back to Auckland we had the time to reflect on a wonderful trip with good companions and a picturesque hunting landscape tempered with its demanding conditions. It was the end of another roar but it had been one that would long be remembered.

Duckville

It was a very pleasant Friday morning, apart from the sandflies, as the three of us lay in the long grass alongside the Horonuinga Base Camp. Lance, Kevin and myself, were supping on some cans of the weekend's supply of snake repellent waiting for Derek and his D Model whirly bird to return from Taupo to lift us into the Duckville bivvy for five days of hunting.

The time was whittled away by yarning to a local lad who was looking for a pig dog that he had lost some weeks before, and about hunting in general. After a time he left, leaving us with the impression that all pig hunters carry scales that register from only 150lbs up. Derek returned just as we were wondering whether or not one of us should pop back into town to

107

restock the snake repellent that had already been consumed. Instead, we piled into the chopper and headed south.

The bivvy was found to be empty and appeared to have been that way for some time. It did not take long to settle in, have some lunch and get ready for an afternoon stalk, each of us taking off in a different direction to suss out the area and report back later.

There was a fair bit of snake repellent used that first night, thus depleting the stocks even further, but it seemed to work really well because we never saw a snake the whole trip. It was also found to work as well on opossums at three in the morning when reprocessed and applied as a warm shower.

Saturday morning arrived and it was time to get serious. I called dibs on the handy spur opposite camp and Lance took off on another to the left while Kevin went to have a look in the valley behind us. Myself, I'm one of those bastards that never learns, as halfway up the nose I was on I decided to stop and give the local stags a yodel, just to let them know I was coming. I rested the 600 up against a handy tree and got the roaring horn tuned up. After my third effort and, puffing on a ciggy with ears twitching for a reply, I was amazed to see a Red stag come running around the track directly at me. He was only about 15 metres away and it was not something for which I had been prepared so late in the roar.

My mouth must have dropped open because my ciggy tumbled to the ground as I wondered how in the hell I was going to take this guy on. Dropping to my knees I scrambled across to my idle firestick, not taking my eyes off the clear little path before me down which the stag was coming. Reaching my rifle I kept at a low crouch — better known as the paddy field prone position — and prepared myself to do wonders on this bugger that no one had told the roar was over.

My attention was then taken by a lot of crashing in thick high ferns above and to the left of me. My first thought was, how in the hell did he get up there, being sure he would have had to cross an area that I had not taken my eyes off for a second. However I was not going to let him get away so I rose to the Quasimodo position and took about four steps along the track with eyes now affixed to the thrashing ferns.

Upon my fifth step I was quickly made aware that I was about to step on the hoof of what appeared in that instant to be a large four pointer stag. So now it dawned on me that I had roared and not one, but two, of the bastards had come running and I had stuffed the whole bloody thing up by not having my cannon handy. I don't know what happened to the one in the ferns, I was too busy trying to deal to the one that was by now some distance off and loudly telling me what he thought of the game I was trying to play, before he too was gone.

So that took care of my Saturday. Lance and Kevin had had a good look around their respective areas and had seen bugger all sign and both returned empty handed. On Sunday Lance spooked two deer but they gave him no chance at a shot and I got a glimpse of four pigs after they got a glimpse of me first.

The creek that acts as access around the block was brim to brim with toetoe grass and stinging nettle with no defined path, but this did not deter my hunting mates as the next morning Kevin went upstream and Lance headed off down. I, on the other hand, played it smart by going back up that ridge where the two stags had been a couple of days earlier.

In the meantime two of the local pig hunters had arrived at the bivvy with a swarm of dogs who proceeded to crap all over the camp. As there were only three bunks in the hut they slept on the floor blocking the doorway and thereby saving the resident opossums from any further treatments of repellant.

One young pup had been badly stung by nettle, its night long whining resulting in a rather sleepless night, so I took the opportunity to head off early the next morning. It was an uneventful tramp back to the top of the spur, until that is, I found myself confronted by a mob of pigs. Three shots later two pigs lay dead, but my immediate thought was that those shots must have sounded pretty evenly spaced, so I let a fourth one off to dispel anyone's idea that there had been a whe te whakamai signal.

Back at the deserted bivvy the pigs were strung up to be attended to later. I collected some firewood and was enjoying a peaceful afternoon nap when Kevin stalked in. He had heard my four 'I'm okay' shots and had also heard another volley from Lance's direction about midday.

The afternoon light started to wane and there was still no sign of Lance so we both went for a stroll downstream to see if we could find him and lend a hand with anything he was trying to carry back. We returned just before dark without sighting him thinking he was going to spend the night in the bush, but he eventually walked in about 30 minutes later to find the pig hunters had already laid claim to his bunk.

He said he had come across a mob of Rusa on a ridge and had bowled two of them over and had then given chase to a bunch of pigs. After that he had spent the rest of the day skinning one of the hinds and ferrying the meat down the ridge and back upstream until he had run out of light, whereupon he had left it where it could be retrieved in the morning.

That final morning was ANZAC day and with Derek due at 11am we had time only to eat, pack and dress up the meat and clean the camp. The two pig hunters and their dogs hung about in the hope that Derek would be able to lift out some of their weekend spoils — they had shot a Rusa and three pigs. But Derek would have nothing to do with them as it was obvious they were in the park illegally and to do so would have dire repercussions for his business.

So an excellent five days was had if you ignore the pig hunters. The bush is good to hunt and animal numbers could be described as moderate, but as far as access goes I definitely recommend the chopper, unless you have a passion for stinging nettle and cutty grass.

Jap Imports

The eastern side of Taupo is dominated by the Kaimanawa Range, which starts as a gentle climb through tea-tree scrub and up to birch forest, and although it is undulating to begin with, it becomes steep with hills rising to 1500 metres. The main range is gullied by rivers and creeks that have cut deep paths through this pumice country. My favourite hunting location in this neck of the woods was a river which ran right through these hills with its birthplace the scoured sides of Ngapuketurua.

Easter weekend saw two of us camped by the Tauranga Taupo river, tucked within the huge valley this waterway had created. The day was one for the album, cold, crisp and clear and in which the stags should have been roaring their heads off. The only snag was we were down by the river and couldn't hear a thing over its thunderous might. So bidding my buddy good luck as we headed in opposite directions I found my first job was a long climb to the top of the ridge.

It was at least 8am before I finally puffed my way to the top and sat down for a well earned rest to listen over the blood drumming in my ears. Not a sound was to be heard from the valley below. Instead, behind my back on the far side of the river big Reds were bellowing, their roars echoing up and down the gorge. Not a single Sika whistled and it was this wily oriental gentleman I had come looking for — and, unlike politicians, they often know when to keep their mouths shut.

It wasn't until mid afternoon that I climbed out of 'Twin Creek Valley' onto a ridge overlooking some bush covered flats. So far I hadn't seen a thing and was becoming a bit despondent. I decided to sit down for a quiet smoke, when suddenly, five long drawn out high-low whistles could be heard from the flats below. Taking a quick compass bearing I started off down the ridge toward this obliging whistler. One of the things I was to learn this trip was that Sika stags, unlike Reds, will often sound off in the afternoon.

It took about half an hour to work my way down to the flats, which were a bit of a misnomer, as it was only the steepness of the hills behind me which made the area seem flat. Once on them I started to worry. The compass bearing I had taken seemed a long time ago, and the stag had stopped being very vocal. Just as I was thinking he had become aware of me he gave voice again confirming I had followed my bearing well. A further 150 metres on and I found the first of his territory holes, with smashed bushes, an obvious wallow and the smell of his urine in the air.

Ten minutes later and I was still wondering where the hell

he was. By this time, I had taken off my boots and was moving fast towards him. My pulse was racing and my mouth was dry. I knew stag fever was rampant and it had a hold of me. It doesn't matter how many times you hunt, this feeling always gets you.

It was a full 20 minutes later before he decided to let the world know that he was the boss in this neck of the woods and this time the whistles sounded long and drawn out, almost like donkey brays. When they get like that you know you're close. He was almost at right angles to where I had first thought him to be, and at most, a couple of hundred metres away. Now I had to watch I didn't scare any of his hinds because if only one of them got wind of me then it would all be over. However there didn't seem to be any breeze and I would just have to take the chance on any eddy carrying my scent over to them.

It was his antler tips I spotted first, on the far side of some low scrub, pure white and highly polished, and as he waved his head from side to side the sun glinted on them. He was half hidden from me, and luckily further away still, were seven hinds and they were all unaware of me.

In those days I used a .303 and the 180 grain bullet was hard hitting. I knew it would only be a matter of time before my scent carried across the divide so I decided to try and hit the stag despite the scrub. I could see his rump and back legs clearly and so that was where I aimed. The first shot took him a little high, because he staggered and lurched into full view. The second shot took him down, hitting him in the back of the neck, and the best Sika I had ever lined up was mine.

I think when I got over to him I let out a bit of a rebel yell because he was even better than I had first thought. Eventually when measured he scored 189 on the 'Douglas' system.

But there is, however, a postscript to this story.

An hour later and back up on top of the ridge where I had started, I was taking a breather, having set the head and skin down beside me. Then, back from where I had just come, a red stag gave a mighty bellow. I decided to reply and he immediately answered so that within a couple of minutes it was obvious he was on his way up to meet me.

It's uncanny how quickly and quietly stags can move, as this one at first had seemed half a mile away. I was peering down the long ridge waiting to see him when he appeared out of a deep gut to my left at a trot. He got to within 10 metres before my nerve broke and I hurriedly put my rifle to my shoulder and let him have one in the chest, dropping him instantly.

Reds in the Kaimanawas do not grow great heads. They're either a poor strain or perhaps there's too much competition from the Japanese Sika. However, this one was a 10 pointer with 33cm brow tines and the best Red head I had seen in these hills. It seemed incredible, but in the space of an hour I had shot the best two heads in 10 years of stalking. It was an Easter to well remember.

Piggy and Gutsy

Being two Auckland deerstalkers who have hunted together for the past three years, we have developed a style of hunting that has given us considerable success. So it seems that an account of one of our recent successful weekend hunts may provide food for thought.

Having stacked our gear in the van with the usual moaning on how little difference there seemed to be between the amount needed for a weekend trip or a week-long trip, and with a few spare dollars in the kitty, we started out on our 300-km drive — a price one pays for living so far from accessible hunting areas.

The weather report had got it right for once as we headed off through the shower-laden day. We missed out on two shapely hitch-hikers just outside of Hamilton by seconds, as a flash car nipped in to pick them up, while our old van was still juddering to a halt. So the only highlight of the drive was a couple of hamburgers from our favourite Rotorua greasy spoon.

After Murapara we tickled the tails of a few opossums, though I'm not prepared to say how, and we finally picked up our permit at the Minginui Forest Headquarters. Then, with the van parked up, we had a quick brew and hit the sack.

We both awoke at daybreak, but it seems there is this unspoken game of let's pretend we're still asleep, at least until 7am, when there is always a mad dash to load our packs and trot off into the bush. Ninety minutes later we were stretching the cover over the frame of our bush shelter and setting up our home comforts.

By 9am, and with a good breakfast under our belts, and heartened by the amount of fresh sign we had seen, Piggy and I started out on our first stalk. Our camp was situated at the base of three ridges that we hunt according to the weather and prevailing wind. It had rained fairly hard during the night and the damp forest floor made the going much quieter. Climbing above the supplejack and into more open beech forest we started our stalking in earnest as we found fresh tracks leading off in all directions.

I kept Piggy in sight by his bright orange cap and the stripes on his Swannee and he likewise. We covered the valley slopes and spurs keeping about 15–20 metres apart but it wasn't until about an hour later, when we came together for a discussion on where to proceed, that we heard a scuffle above us.

Piggy spotted an old hind with a yearling in front of her which he dropped straight away. All the more satisfying as we were both using ammunition we had reloaded at a bench rest evening a couple of weeks before. It always seems more rewarding when you bowl something over with your own ammunition.

With the hind skinned and boned out we decided to hunt the other side of the ridge back to camp. The rain had held off for all of that morning but as we turned back it started to fall so we hurried along.

About 10 minutes or so later we spotted two more hinds moving slowly through the trees about 20 metres above us. Picking the leading hind as she stopped to try and make out where we were, I let fly. Instead of dropping, she charged straight down past us and it took a second shot to finish her.

With a deer each to carry and the rain starting to really pour down we headed back for camp. We were almost there when, over the rise, came a dark coloured stag, wet and bedraggled and looking very uncomfortable. After a few hoots and whistles from us he ambled off up and over the next ridge.

Arriving at camp we made a welcome brew and relived the shooting of our hinds a few dozen times until we had ridden that conversation into the ground. Looking at our watches we saw there were still a few hours before dinner. 'Time for a quick stalk?' said Piggy, though I knew he wasn't all that serious and instead we both fell for the old snooze-before-tucker trick. After the nap we set to and went about producing and devouring the kind of spread that has given us both our nicknames.

For our Sunday morning stalk we decided on the largest ridge behind camp, but on clearing the supplejack the wind kept veering around behind us. So I settled down for a half hour to allow Piggy to circle around and climb up the ridge to where there are some open areas.

The mist was lifting with blue sky showing through when I

started to work over to where I knew Piggy was waiting. The deer unfortunately didn't co-operate and fresh tracks were as near as we could get. So, splitting up, we started to work the small fuchsia gullies running down the northern side of the ridge.

With the mist cleared and the sun shining, the bush looked like a different place. As I slowly worked my way down the valley I counted over 10 shots coming from the flats. So with my mind on this and other things it was too late when I finally spotted a large hind walking quietly into the bush below and on the other side of the gully.

She must have watched me for some time before moving off. Crouching down I followed her through the scope as she headed up towards me. The bush was too thick for a shot but I was sure there would be a chance for one when she crossed above me. But with that knack they seem to have, she trotted across at a point where there was still too much bush in the way.

I decided to call it a day after having a deer literally run rings around me and made it back to camp to find that Piggy hadn't faired any better. So, striking camp, we headed out with the reassuring weight of a successful trip on our backs and the knowledge that the camp we had grown to think of as a second home will still be there for the next time . . . and the next.

Walton's Mountain

Jim and I pulled to a stop alongside the D Model at the appointed hour of 9am on that Friday morning in Murupara to find Derek giving the machine a spit polish. I don't know who he was trying to impress because it sure wasn't us. We were only half expecting to get into one of our pet spots because of the weather, but according to Derek, there wasn't going to be a problem.

Now Waltons Mountain, as we had named it, is very high and it seems to have its own weather system, especially if the wind is anywhere from the southerly quarter. There is always the possibility of being put down there and having the weather close in on you, preventing the helicopter from returning to lift you out again on the appointed time and day.

There were a few moments when I thought we were not going to make it because the mist and cloud percolating over the main ridge looked like cotton wool but, soon enough, there was the hut directly beneath us. Since there were only the two of us on this trip we had managed to stow all our gear for the next three days inside long before the sound of the chopper had faded from ear shot.

A quick inspection of the hut revealed that not one soul had visited the place since my last trip some three months earlier. It's a rare chance to return to a camp site and get to burn the firewood you replaced before leaving the last time. It took about an hour to set up camp, have a brew, and make ready to take the firestick for a walk.

An initial reconnaissance of the area began with me bringing up the rear behind Jim when somehow I found myself on my own. Coming to a sort of crossroads near the top of the ridge system, I decided to hang a left into some country I have never yet hunted but always had an inkling to cover. The wind this day was not entirely suitable but I decided to push on and check it out anyway.

The first couple of hundred metres were a boggy mess but it soon opened out into some nice stalking country and I managed to quietly sneak up into two very old camp sites, which rather spoilt the feeling that I was breaking virgin ground. A little over an hour later a light drizzle had turned into a steady rain so I turned for home.

Jim, it turned out, had dropped off the side of the ridge unnoticed by me, which explained how we had become separated. We had both seen plenty of fresh sign and it had our hopes high for the next day. That evening the potbelly was stoked up to air out our wet gear, though this made life uncomfortably hot, so the door was left open, which, in turn, attracted clouds of moths around the lantern. The bloody things became so profuse that Jim spent a solid hour trying to repel the hordes before fashioning himself a suit of armour from an old newspaper.

That night was a restless one as the local opossums decided to hold a disco on the hut roof and rearrange the firewood in the bin just outside the door. Sunday, when it came, was cloudy with strong winds and I left Jim to go his way while I went to climb Waltons Mountain once more. This time the wind was totally wrong for that left turn so I carried on straight ahead. From my perch, the odd break in the cloud revealed that it was a fine and clear day far below in Ruatahuna.

I returned to the hut some time around 10.30am with a young hind that was, surprisingly, still in her winter coat and strung her up to attend to later. Jim was there to give me a hand. He had been for a big stalk and seen plenty of fresh sign but had come away without any luck. After a couple of beers (Aussies call it XXXX because they can't spell beer) and a feed it was firewood time again. We spent an hour cutting and chopping at a wind fallen tree on the other side of the helipad. We then carted armfuls up until the bin was full with another large pile stacked alongside the track.

With that chore completed we decided it was time for another stalk and I headed off along the track beside the firewood. I had it firmly in mind that I would need to put in a good 10 minutes of quick tramping down the path before I could even begin to hunt as I was sure all the commotion and hilarity of the wood chopping would have cleared the area of any prize.

Imagine my surprise then when only 50 metres down the track two deer scampered for safety, one of which began barking over and over at me from the tight rubbish off and up to the left. Knowing I was trying to push shit up hill by going in after it I went anyway, but as expected, came up with nothing. Retracing my steps I saw that, had I been concentrating on my way down the track, I should've been able to spot the animals before they bolted.

I returned to the hut to enjoy the place and to relax while Jim, as usual, prepared the evening meal. We had brought along steak and kidney but he seemed to get a little carried away and added the venison liver and kidneys, creating this huge pot of grub we had no way in hell of finishing ourselves. We kept going to the door and yelling out, 'Tea is ready! Come and get it!' But no one showed up and I rather imagine the opossums dined very well on it the next night.

The following morning we were packed and ready, though the weather did not look the best for Derek to show up, and we wondered if we would be unpacking our gear again for an unplanned stay. But around 11am we heard the whop-whop-whop of the chopper approaching. After a bit of a yarn and the usual cuppa we were back in Murupara and turning our eyes homeward, and already thinking about our next trip.

Stewart Island

Sleep was hard to find, even with the soft patter of a light rain on the tent fly, when your hunting budding was snoring his head off next to you like a chainsaw chomping through tea tree. And in the background of this unholy noise were the distant booming and raucous retorts of stags high up in the valley that gave me the thrill of anticipation for tomorrow's hunt. When sleep finally did overcome me, it was to the sound of those stags whose roars rolled across the ridges.

The next day found me at dawn among the rushes and flax, with a heavy bog underfoot through which I had to plough, becoming quickly drenched by the dripping head high tangle of foliage. The rain had stopped hours ago but it might as well have been still pouring down, so quickly did I become soaked to the bone. I paused to take a look at a high bush clad ridge that extended away from me, starting at the swollen stream I was following and stretching up and up until it disappeared into a grey mist. This was where the Reds had been bellowing, straight opposite our campsite where we had decided to pitch our tents after the long trek from Long Harry Bay.

I searched for a way around or across the seemingly endless meandering sea-bound stream, becoming somewhat frustrated, and was almost tempted to try and plough straight through it. But I kept recalling the story of a hunter who had gone missing in this very area. It was told that his dog, when asked to find his master, would go no further than a stretch of quicksand where he sat down on its edge and whined. I had no inclination to suffer such a fate.

After the raucous sounds of the night before, this morning sounded very still and serene with only the muted rumbling of the distant surf reaching me through the reeds. I also noted that the sun had now pushed the cloud back and was touching the ridge tops giving me a sense of urgency as I imagined the stags now beginning to bed down for the day. A sound reached out to me from that ridge, a mournful moan that brought my plunging steps to a halt.

It was the last straw that would have me tempting fate. I left the stream, pushing back the flax and tramping down a path over which I could get a running start. Then, bracing myself, I headed straight at the water and leapt headlong from the sand-bank. Bubbles oozed out of the sand all around and popped to the surface with a lazy gurgling sound. I heaved myself at the opposite side to grab at the rushes and with a great sigh of relief pulled myself up onto the bank.

With the frightful sound of the stream still bubbling away behind me I pushed my way through the flax to finally find myself in a stand of tea tree which would take me up to the ridge. A pair of tui chased each other with a loud flapping of wings and whooshing noise as they ducked and dived. They left me as quickly as they had appeared and once more I stood in total silence.

I stopped when I reached the first knoll and tried to quiet my breath and the sound of blood in my ears as I strained to listen for the hint of a roar. The ridge began to narrow as I resumed climbing, its seaward side dropping very sharply into sunlight, while on the other side lay a dark and gloomy gully. I stopped again, listened and then cupped my hands around my mouth and gave a long low roar.

A reply was given almost immediately, but it was faint and distant and very high above me. It sounded as if he was up at the very head of the gully, so to get a better pinpoint of his location I roared again. He obligingly replied, so with renewed energy I began climbing once more, the aches in my legs now forgotten.

A big tree sat at the top of a knoll with a huge buttressed root system that seemed to hold onto the whole of the ridge and over which I had to climb. Coming around the tree and onto a small flattened area from which a trail led in and out I stopped to give another roar. Hardly had the sound passed my lips than a challenging bellow boomed out. It was so close that I froze in immobility. Then again he roared and I knew he was coming in for a fight.

I dropped down behind one of the massive tree roots focusing my eyes on the two paths before me wondering which of these he would appear in. Then with a booming roar and a thrashing of antlers he crashed his way down the path on the left. I had to rise to swing the rifle in his direction and he immediately spotted me and jerked sideways.

His bulk filled the scope from only about 3 metres away and I pulled the trigger. I saw a blur of red and made to load another round, but it wasn't needed. His legs buckled and he toppled from the ridge, sliding about 20 metres down the bank. When I reached him, his head was turned sideways showing just one antler of five points, I had to twist him around to count the other side which showed only four points. But it was still a nice head and one that holds great memories of a time well spent on Stewart Island.

The Nearly Record

I was sitting on top of the world, or so it seemed, as the clouds drifted by some 300 metres below me. My view of this vast panorama seemed hardly possible to surpass. To my left lay a series of broken ridges, reaching down like long tentacles to a river which appeared as a thin pencil line in the distance. To my right was a majestic peak a further 250 metres above me. However, without having any mountain climbing experience, and with limited tackle, I settled for where I was and waited for my cobber John, who was approaching our rendezvous point from a different angle. Another half hour passed before he appeared.

He explained that the extra time he had taken on his way up the eastern ridge was because he had come across a bunch of

Chamois. He detoured across the face to get a little closer to them and in doing so ran into a very fine billy. When it saw him it took off, raising the alarm, and the rest of the mob scattered too. He followed them for a time but whenever a possible chance presented itself for a shot it turned out to be one of the lesser beasts, that were well below trophy standard.

I opened my pack and offered him some stale bread and cheese which he ate with gusto and then looked for more. We'd had a hearty breakfast that morning but climbing 1500 metres was enough to work up anyone's appetite. We sat for a time pondering over the game that each of us had seen and decided that the billy John had encountered was the best trophy head spotted so far on this trip.

So, with our minds made up, we sauntered off in the direction we thought the Chamois would take, thinking that we would be very lucky if we were to make contact with them again. We had been going for about 2 hours, in which we had not covered a great deal of country, when John noticed some movement about 700 metres away. I lifted the binoculars over to the area he was pointing to and focused upon the best Chamois head I had ever seen.

'Well it's your head John, if you can get him,' I said.

It was all the prompting he needed and I sat down to watch as he edged from cover to cover trying to close the gap to a shootable distance with the tension mounting as he closed in. The big Chamois was in a group of five and they were all unaware that their only enemy was now but a few hundred yards away.

John worked himself down onto a small shelf in readiness to take his shot which appeared to be from about 300 metres. The billy, as if at last sensing that all was not as it should be, stood up tall and took a long and hard stare in his direction. Then with the grace of a gazelle he bounded up onto a large rock, perhaps for a better view of his surroundings, and afforded John an ideal shot, who wasted no time in firing.

I saw the billy go down well before the shot reached my ears. He was hit perfectly and he slid down the rock face coming to rest before the last of the echoes had died away. The other Chamois bounded off and John let them go, happy with what he had achieved. We took the cape skin and head from the animal and began the long march back to camp very satisfied with our prize.

Later on the head was measured and, although it didn't break any records, it did come very very close.

With Satay Sauce

Now cotton wool is real handy stuff. It has many uses; there are cotton balls, cotton buds and cotton wads for all those important little places. But when it comes to flying through cotton wool in a bloody helicopter with the pilot hanging out the hole in the machine where the door ought to be for 'better visibility', you seem to temporarily lose your sense of flamin' humour.

Therein lies the guts of this tale of our trip into our favourite hunting block for the next four nights. After the departure of the machine the rain came down in earnest and most of the remainder of that day was spent just spreading ourselves out in the hut and getting comfortable.

Now none of us could in any way be called 'spring chickens'

and a quick add up of our combined ages totalled 182 years. I should imagine that represents quite a few pounds of hot lead spread about the countryside over that time, not to mention all the flamin' bullshite that goes with it.

The wood box, as per usual, had been left pretty much empty by the hut's previous visitors and, with everything dripping wet outside, that particular chore was put on hold until the following day. Leo was to take charge of the firewood detail with his axe 'Excalibre'. Although his knife gets called Excalibre and his rifle Excalibre too, we vocally doubted his wife had anything she could call Excalibre.

The following day was fine and clear with a very light north westerly and I had an undeniable urge to check out ridge 9 which has a happy habit of producing stags in the early mornings, especially after rain. This particular ridge has two patches of bare high ground under a full canopy of bush. It seems to be a favourite spot for deer to sun themselves away from the wet undergrowth.

I approached the first patch from an awkward angle due to the light breeze that was drifting in from slightly behind me and off to my right. It would certainly have warned any game that Armageddon was on its way, so I was forced into this approach. I got to a position where I could see a little over half of the patch and stood frozen there for a while with my ears flapping for any hint of a sound and my nose twitching for the scent of a deer. I let my eyes study, over and over, the ground ahead but the clearing held no hint of a deer.

There was a broken, wind fallen log, one end of which I could see poking out from behind another tree about 15 metres ahead. If one used one's imagination you could say it looked like the rear end of a deer. I raised the rifle scope just to check it out. 'Nope.' It was a log alright but one could easily have been fooled by it.

Putting the rifle down I continued to just stand there looking and listening. Looking back at the log I thought I saw it give a twitch. Up came the scope again and I studied the thing once more, this time for quite awhile, but obviously my eyes were deceiving me and my fervent imagination was running away on me.

Down came the rifle once more and still I continued to stand there motionless. I remember thinking that there would be the odd hunter who might have pumped a round into that log and then would have returned to camp and explained away his actions. But not me mate, not today, not bloody likely. I'd never live an action like that down, not after all these years in this game.

I was about to move on when I got the distinct impression that the bit in the centre of that log end, that bit that looked so much like a tail, gave another flick. Now this time I didn't bother to lift the rifle, instead I just rocked on the balls of my feet and leaned over slightly and slowly to the left.

'Holly bloody makerel,' I thought as, into view, came an ear and then an antler of a stag looking back over its shoulder in my direction. It couldn't see me because of the intervening tree. Now in years gone by I would probably have tried to get myself into a position where I could place my shot a bit better, and if everything went as it usually did, I would have stuffed the whole thing up and missed out completely.

Not any more mate, these days I just take what I can get and if the meat gets a bit stuffed up in the process, well I just have to live with it. Some meat is better than none as far as I'm concerned.

My first shot at his rump took out his mobility and it took another two shots (the first of which was a miss) before I hit him in the neck and the rest was history. The main thing was we would have meat back at camp and the trip was off to a great start.

I arrived back at the hut with the spoils of my morning hunt to find Ron and Leo hard at work cutting firewood to the accompaniment of aged huffs, puffs, wheezes, moans and groans. But, in no time at all, the wood box was full again and the decision was made then and there that roast venison was on the menu for the following evening.

Sadly, the next day of hunting, as with the remaining days, turned out to be unproductive. There were stags around, and they would answer a roar from a hunter, but that was it. They would not keep going on their own to give their hunter more than a general idea of their whereabouts. There were also others that would get all upset when disturbed and head for hidden places, grunting and barking as they disappeared.

The roast dinner, as it turned out, was one of the features of the trip. The entree was oyster fritters garnished with tomato sauce. The main was roast venison accompanied by roast spuds, carrots and onions plus peas and beans with satay sauce. Dessert was apricot halves, and the dishes . . . well they waited until the next morning.

The Party Hunt

There was one year when a branch of the NZDA was not getting the support of its members in efforts to provide meat for the Annual Dinner, and with this dinner only a short time away it was decided that the executive members should go out into the hills in search of some venison. The party assembled at the home of the president and proceeded to cram into all the available space of two vehicles with a conglomeration of packs, lilos, gas stoves, food, boots, rifles and a dog. What space was left was taken up by eight men and a boy. With a cheery call of 'See you at Timberlands', the first of the vehicles set off, closely followed by the second, in a roar and surge of power.

After some miles the party had settled into their comfortable positions when the healthy roar under the bonnet of the Land Rover was replaced with the silence one associates with travel in a Rolls Royce. This particular silence, however, was accompanied by a rapid deceleration causing considerable angst amongst the passengers. After everyone had had a fiddle, the trouble was finally located as a broken wire from the condenser. Luckily our ever-prepared treasurer produced a replacement and we were once again back under way.

One hundred and fifty kilometres further on and our journey was once again disrupted, this time by the rapid exit of air from our back tyre. Whilst changing the wheel in a fairly thick fog the party was very nearly cleaned out by two cars travelling too close together and too fast for the conditions. There was a mad rush for the grass verge as the headlights bore down on us and swept by far too close for comfort. Once our hearts had stopped pounding and our knees stopped knocking the wheel change was finished and we continued on to Taupo where we removed the tube from the tyre. It came out in many small pieces.

The last leg of the journey after this was thankfully uneventful, apart from one point where we ended up going sideways down a track as the front wheels set into one set of ruts and the rear wheels slid into another. We also had to push the first vehicle up a hill on a washed-out pumice track before finally hitting camp at about 2 o'clock in the morning in a heavy frost and biting cold.

Four or five shivering hours later we arose and, after a hearty and welcome breakfast, split up into small groups to set off in search of some sleeping deer. But the deer, it appeared, were very much awake and already on the move.

The president, a chap called Ron, saw the first deer as it ran across a bush track. He pursued it at great speed and failed to see in his path a small Sika stag. Both he and the stag must have been very surprised as Ron ended up almost on top of it. It turned to run and obligingly tripped over a fallen branch allowing Ron to shoot it just as though he had known it was there all the time. He insists however that he was intending to catch the animal bare handed. This happened on the left of a gully where the secretary, Brian and the boys were hunting.

On the right, two quick shots were heard. It turned out to be Bill who, with Bob, was heading across country to a place called Third Creek. A deer made the mistake of crossing the track in front of them and lingered long enough for Bill to pull the trigger twice on his autoloader, and presto, meat for the pot.

The secretary and his group looked around an awful lot of corners and into a lot of gullies, but everywhere this group went, the deer had been and gone. Late in the day all parties arrived home with a total of four deer, and a splendid meal was had in the comfort of a canvas bivvy with liver, kidney, fillet steak, potatoes and tinned fruit. Also, mention should be made of one chap named Les whose ability to knock over a boiling tea-billy with a clumsy size 11 boot, not only once but twice, saw him banished to the corner.

The next day the groups set out again, but this time with different people. The president led a party in search of a deer that had been shot the day before and hung in a tree. To some it looked like being a search for a needle in a haystack, but after several wrong turns they walked right on top of it, which seemed rather a good effort considering the nature of the country where every gully looks the same.

On this day Bill, Bob and Brian set out with a pack, food, sleeping bags and a tent. They intended to spend the night out in the bush and hunt back in the morning. Something went wrong, however, and although they did spend the night out, Brian, who was on the wrong side of the ridge when darkness fell, spent the night by himself, without a tent.

He was the last back to camp on the day of our return having come out on the road several miles from camp. The secretary and the boy set out to inspect a patch of bush that had yet to be hunted – at least that was their intention – but their sense of direction turned out to have a bend in it and they too came out in the wrong place.

The lie of the land in this area is very deceiving and whilst travelling it is very easy to stray from one's intended direction. Constant use of a compass is most necessary, not just a cursory glance every hour, as was the case with this group.

The total score for the three days was six deer which was not bad when one considers that 19 hunters were in the area. The secretary, as usual, did not spoil his average of no shots fired for no deer. But, all things considered, it was an enjoyable weekend and the meat taken back ensured that the Annual Dinner had fresh venison and not mutton.

Chicken Wire and Builder's Paper

'We'll be there at 9am Friday morning,' I had told Derek, and it was but one minute past when we drove up his driveway and parked by the chopper that had a large pile of opossum skins and trappers gear sitting next to it.

'Just came out of the Waiau,' said the young trapper. 'Yeah and there are a few deer in there but you have to look for them.'

So what's new? I thought.

Our last view of the lad as we took off was of him sitting in the cab of his Holden still trying to start it with a flat battery. Most of his skins and gear were blasted up against Derek's deer fence by the draft of the D-Model's blades.

Fifteen minutes later, and on his second approach, Derek put us down in a puddle that served as the chopper pad for the

Te Rangaakapua Bivvy. It was a place that none of us had ever seen or heard of before, but it came highly recommended, so here we were, Dave, Jim, Ian and myself. The bivvy sported three bunks and was constructed of malthoid, chicken wire and builders paper – there was no fireplace. It was decided that we would each take a turn sleeping on the floor and, as we were in for three nights, it meant that Jim's turn was next.

The usual poke around revealed that there was no meat safe for any kill and that little remained of what had originally been the 'bog'. It too had been constructed of malthoid, but two of its walls had given up the struggle during some past storm, or perhaps the overwhelming number of blowflies had merely knocked it down. Needless to say the bloody thing had also been constructed in the middle of the track to the Makakoere Stream, and whenever anyone used it there was always this conscious fear of someone coming walking around the corner.

That first afternoon Dave and I explored the ridge to the north while Jim and Ian had a look to the south. We found that the slatted track we had been using took a sudden dive off the ridge towards the east but from our vantage point the country down there looked inviting, so off we went. Down however was the operative word, and after about 40 minutes of clambering over many a wind-fallen log, we saw that the next track marker could be seen at quite a drop straight below us.

Now I have had my turn at hoisting beasties out of some bloody awful spots, and my view on the matter was that I have been there and done that. Besides, there was little deer sign about and it was beginning to hail. I looked at Dave, and I looked down into the drop, and then I looked back at Dave. 'I could do with a brew,' I said. I think he suppressed the desire to hug me at that point as I basically suggested we pack it in and head back.

Returning to the bivvy we heard that Ian had put up a stag while Jim had merely done an uneventful poke around. Saturday morning Ian and I took off to hunt our way down to the Mangatoatoa Hut about three hours away. Dave would go back in the direction of the previous day, but instead of following the track down would ignore it and carry on along the ridge where some encouraging deer sign had been seen. Jim was left in bed.

Ian and I returned that afternoon from a marathon stalk where we had sighted just two deer. Jim and Dave were relaxing outside the bivvy in the warm sun and all, but blocking the doorway was the head of a four pointer. It turned out that Dave had spotted the animal from some distance away and had moved in on it quietly, taking his time to get close enough to knock it over with his 6mm.

This was Dave's first deer after many trips away and it came as a welcome piece of news to us all. Tinnies were handed all around and the order of the day was to relax.

On Sunday piles of fresh sign were found but not one sighting to be had by any of us. Derek was due in with the chopper at 11am on Monday but as he had been early coming to get us on other occasions, we knew not to stray too far from the hut, electing instead to tidy up around the bivvy.

The flight back to Murupara was made in brilliant weather making even the Labour Day traffic seem bearable as we headed for home.

Imagine that . . .

Now we've all heard those fishy tales about the one that got away. It's always a monster with the fisherman holding his arms wide to show just how large it was. Well it seems the same stories abound for deer hunters and for missed stags, which are usually of mammoth proportions, with 12 points, bounding through the bush at 300 metres.

Have you ever shot a deer at 300 metres in the bush? What about the big stag frequenting the same area each roar? Usually a hunter friend always sees him and remembers every detail about the great set of antlers he has but somehow never has time for a shot. Then one day somebody else shoots him and he's found to be not a bad head but certainly not the trophy winning standard he was described as. So immediately the cry will go out that he's not the one and that the monster must still reside in those bush clad hills.

I remember a classic example of this when on a trip into the Te Iringa. Two of us arrived at a hut just on dark and settled in for the night, then at around 10pm the sound of footsteps was heard approaching and two young chaps walked in. So the fire was restoked and a general chinwag began. It seems these boys had been in on the previous weekend and one of them shot at, but missed, a stag. On being asked whether it was a Red or a Sika the immediate reply was, 'A huge Red stag with a big head.' The indication he gave of the size of the body and antlers didn't add up in that particular area and as it was only the second week of February it was highly likely to still be in full velvet anyway.

When asked about the velvet the hunter was adamant that there was no velvet and that the antlers were polished up. Later in the evening they confessed to us that this was only their second hunting trip and the stag of the previous weekend was the first deer either of them had ever seen in the wild. The next morning they left camp to follow the Tiki Tiki stream.

On Sunday afternoon we met them again on our way out to the car.

'How did you get on?' we asked.

'Found the stag I thought I had missed last week,' said one.

'Oh yeah, what was it like?'

'A seven pointer,' they replied.

'What? A Red?'

'No a Jap.'

'Big?'

'About so big,' said one holding his hands apart to show a small head.

'So did you bring it out?'

143

'No it had gone rotten. It was in velvet and crawling with maggots.'

Perhaps these lads could be excused, as it was their first deer, but it just goes to show how the stories never add up to the reality. I'll bet there are a lot of older hunters too who still imagine those big stags. The ones that get away and must wait for another day, with 12 points on a massive trophy winning head, bounding away through the bush at 300 metres. Imagine that.

Big Red

'See you at 10am outside the Tarawera boozer,' Peter had said. 'And bring plenty of camping gear with ya.'

Now those who have been away hunting with me know that I needn't ever be told that I seem to find room for everything, even a kitchen sink, once. This particular weekend my mate Jim and I were off to check out the Tataraakina Block run by Eastern Bay Trappers. Jim has a crook hip though he did have a hip replacement operation many years ago, but the thing has since packed up and needs redoing. Hence he usually has trouble wandering further than a good six iron from the hut.

Peter said to leave some room in the back of the van and he would lend us a 4x4 bike for Jim to poke around on, as the area is honeycombed with old logging tracks. So after a short wait at Tarawera, a chap called Roger Unsworth cruised up with a trailer in tow on which sat a big red Honda quad bike. The drill was now to remove the bike from the trailer and then hook the trailer to the bike and stow the gear from the van onto the trailer. From there we would sit in tandem and roar off into the mist and gloom towards Wakemans Clearing.

The initial part of this particular journey went well enough because it was an easy jalopy ride along smooth quite reasonable farm track up to the bush line. After a while Jim reckoned he had worked out what Tataraakina meant in Maori – 'The farm of many gates,' he said. But we were soon surrounded by bush and scrub and after going through one last big steel gate, which we locked behind us, we set off for the camp site. We had clattered our way along until our first big test appeared before us. We had come to the top of a big downhill run. Now I'm not saying it was steep, it's just that you had to lean forward and look down over your front two tyres to see where you were steering.

'I'll get off aye?' said Jim. Not bloody likely I thought. If I go, he's coming with me.

'She'll be right, stay where you are,' I replied and off we went. I can only say that I was completely and utterly impressed with the way that big old 4x4 bike performed, both on that run, and during the rest of the weekend. There seemed to be nowhere it wouldn't go with two large men aboard and a light road trailer with a ton of gear in tow.

It was about an hour later, and one filled with hilarity, that we found ourselves outside Moose Creek Hut, a building that remains standing, left over from the long-past logging era. It was here that we had decided to camp for the weekend. Now I'll not turn this into a drawn out hunting yarn, nor bore you by describing the masses of deer that were seen and shot,

146

because there were none. Just one opossum that made the nights a misery.

On the way home we did encounter a Traffic Officer who could see no humour in the trailer that was returning to Taupo. He couldn't have been worried about the registration that wasn't, or the number plate it didn't have, or the lights that didn't work. But I did get the distinct impression that somehow I had made his day.

But never mind that. The thing is, I now have a brand new love affair, with a big red Honda 4x4 bike. So take a tip from me and whenever you go hunting from now on, make sure you've got a Big Red between your legs.

Reflections

Now I have been away on one or two (hundred) hunting trips in my time, the first of which was into the original old Lochinver Station when it was all tussock and tea tree mate. The year was 1949 and ever since that time there have been quite a few unforgettable events happen.

For instance, on that first trip we had a choice of two pumice caves in which to camp. The first, and best of the two, had only recently been vacated by a bunch of deer cullers and the site had been left a bloody disaster area littered with cans, bottles and all kinds of indescribable rubbish, most of which was covered in flies.

The second cave was much smaller, and one where you had to stoop once inside, unless, that is, you were a 14-year short arse like myself. It was chosen by the grown ups who did not fancy all the cleaning out that the first cave would have required, and besides, we were only going to be spending one night in there anyway.

That night I was woken by pumice being sprinkled on my face and someone shaking the hell out of my bed. But as it happened I was sleeping on the ground and came to the realisation that we were in the middle of an earthquake and the pumice was falling from the roof. When daylight came it was revealed that the first cave had collapsed and, had we decided to spend the night in there, I imagine we would have been buried, and remain so to this day.

On another trip, George, one of my cuzzies, was given a list of meat to get from the butcher's shop in Te Kawa. He had been asked to get 4lbs of sausages. Buggered if I know how, but 4lbs turned into 14lbs and we had sausages coming out our ears on our way home from that trip. I remember that it took a full day of travel, each way, in a 1930 Model A Ford truck from Te Awamutu to Poronui Station. Things sure have changed a bit.

Incidentally, that trip was into Merrilees Clearing in 1950 and there were deer and wild horses everywhere. My Uncle Dick shot a pig from inside the hut through the back of the fireplace . . . and my ears are still ringing. The pig, boar or sow, I can't remember now, was rubbing itself against the warm tin after we had gone to bed. I was sleeping on the floor in front of the fire when the scraping noise started. He let strip with his old .303 (that was the magic calibre in those days, in fact, it was the only calibre) over the top of me and I can remember being covered from arsehole to afternoon tea with ash, sparks and charcoal.

On another trip into the same spot years later, the four of us went into an old Plateau Hut (R.I.P) in the middle of winter, only to find that upon arrival yours truly had left his flamin' sleeping bag at home. Guess who sat up for two whole nights stoking the fire and keeping the hut so warm that the other occupants slept on top of their sleeping bags while it snowed outside.

Then there was a trip into Lake Waikaremoana. One of the party was an idiot called Richard whom I asked to go and fetch me a billy of water. He returned about 15 minutes later covered in hook grass, leaves and assorted other rubbish with half a pot full of muck that you would not give to your pigs. I asked him where the hell he had got it and was told he had bush bashed a trail up the gutter behind camp to find a muddy little stream where he tried to fill the pail.

I pointed in front of me and said, 'You know there is a 75-square-kilometre pool of fresh water we call a lake not 10 paces from here. Why not get it out of there?'

I don't remember his reply, I don't think he was listening anyway. Then there was his interminable question: 'Are there any goats around here?' I got so sick and tired of answering, 'No!' that the joker came as close as anyone ever did to walking home. I still get the cold fuzzies when I think back on that guy. His name may well have been Richard but it wasn't too long before he became known as Dick to the whole camp.

More recently I had an experience in which we were flown in by chopper and just 20 minutes after the machine had departed discovered I had left the bulk of the food back at home in the beer fridge . . . what an idiot. A quick search of what we did have revealed one can of baked beans and one of spaghetti, a loaf of bread, some cup-o-soups, a pot of jam and some onions and spuds.

Later, more spuds were found to be growing in the rubbish

hole out the back of the hut. We also uncovered some pepper, salt and tomato sauce sachets, a tin of mushrooms and, wonder of wonders, a tin of corned beef. So the evening meal consisted of baked beans liberally garnished with fried onions. Now as scavenger meals go it was bloody nice but I'm sure you can imagine the consequences of baked beans and fried onions once digested. I don't know how many times the bog door scraped open and slammed shut in the wee small hours of that night. Needless to say, those items were never again to appear on the menu.

Breakfast on the last morning of that trip was a pretty sparse affair, so that when we hit Rotorua we dined out on steak and egg burgers, chips, battered fish, fritters and sausages. Though there were only the two of us, the cook seemed to think we were taking our families out for a picnic.

Glossary

Bach – Holiday abode
Bangers – Sausages
Billy – Campfire cooking pot
Bivvy – Camp shelter (from 'bivouac')
Bog – Toilet
Brekky – Breakfast
Brew – Cup of tea
Bumpf – Small bits and pieces
Ciggy – Cigarette
Clobber – Outfit
Cobber – Friend, mate
Cutty Grass – A species of sedge with sharp serrated leaves
Cuzzies – Cousins
Dibs – Claim the rights to
Dunny – Toilet
Kaka – Native bird
Pharter – Backside
Rubber neckers – On lookers
Slog – Tiring walk
Snake repellent – Beer
Snarlers – Sausages
Starkers – Naked
Swanni – Swanndri, a bushman's jacket
Tinbum – One who has success without effort
Tucker – Meal
Weka – Native bird
Whe te whakamai – translated as 'Where the f##k am I?'

Made in the USA
Monee, IL
16 March 2022

92977115R00085